D1572658

LOST RACE OF THE
GIANTS

"The fact that the red-haired giants of pre-Columbian America introduced agriculture to our continent is an established, if generally unrecognized, archaeological fact. No one tells their story better than Patrick Chouinard."

FRANK JOSEPH, AUTHOR OF *BEFORE ATLANTIS*,
THE LOST CIVILIZATION OF LEMURIA, AND
ADVANCED CIVILIZATIONS OF PRE-HISTORIC AMERICA

LOST RACE ^{OF} ^{THE}
GIANTS

THE MYSTERY OF THEIR CULTURE, INFLUENCE, AND DECLINE THROUGHOUT THE WORLD

PATRICK CHOUINARD

Bear & Company
Rochester, Vermont • Toronto, Canada

Bear & Company
One Park Street
Rochester, Vermont 05767
www.BearandCompanyBooks.com

Bear & Company is a division of Inner Traditions International

Library of Congress Cataloging-in-Publication Data
Chouinard, Patrick.
  Lost race of the giants : the mystery of their culture, influence, and decline
throughout the world / Patrick Chouinard.
      p. cm.
  Includes bibliographical references and index.
  Summary: "An exploration of mythological and archaeological evidence for
prehistoric giants"—Provided by publisher.
  ISBN 978-1-59143-148-0 (pbk.) — ISBN 978-1-59143-833-5 (e-book)
  1. Giants. 2. Civilization, Ancient. I. Title.
  GR560.C48 2013
  599.9'49—dc23
                                                                    2013006941

Printed and bound in the United States by Lake Book Manufacturing, Inc.
The text stock is SFI certified. The Sustainable Forestry Initiative® program
promotes sustainable forest management.

10 9 8 7 6 5 4 3 2 1

Text design and layout by Brian Boynton
This book was typeset in Garamond Premier Pro with Candara and Myriad Pro as
display typefaces

To send correspondence to the author of this book, mail a first-class letter to the
author c/o Inner Traditions • Bear & Company, One Park Street, Rochester, VT
05767, and we will forward the communication, or contact the author directly at
mythsofatlantis2@gmail.com.

This book is warmly dedicated to my uncle,
William "Monty" Montgomery.

CONTENTS

Giants and the Search for Higher Intelligence

PAUL VON WARD

Over the last few decades millions of people have begun to realize that our academic history books are filled with holes and patched with misleading conclusions based on flimsy evidence. The human story programmed into the minds of today's high school and college graduates is now being proven false in very fundamental ways.

Ironically, scholars in our major research and scientific institutions whose roles include discovering the true story of our past have not initiated these revelations. Instead, the intellectual movement to more accurately reconstruct ancient history has been led by independent, interdisciplinary scholars such as Erich von Däniken, the late Zecharia Sitchin, and a growing number of others—including Patrick Chouinard. Books by these authors focus on discoveries that reveal gaps in standard history books. They also reexamine the academic assertion that ancient texts must be seen as myths or metaphors instead of descriptions of real events. Chouinard's scholarly evaluation of new and old discoveries turns so-called myths into historical narratives.

Books based largely on intuition about the myth of a lost Atlantean era in the human past are often as mystical as the legend itself. In this book, however, Chouinard presents tangible evidence to help fill the "Atlantis gap"—perhaps one hundred thousand years or more—in the documented history of Earth and its humanoid inhabitants.

This book is significant for seekers, skeptics, and believers because it grounds many legends and myths in real-world events, providing authentication of the tales about giants. The evidence that giants were historical beings is proof that many ancient texts must now be seen as valid, if partial, historical documents. Chouinard's investigations mean we can no longer view Hebrew, Christian, Islamic, or other religious documents referring to "giants of old" as divine descriptions of other realms. Neither can we label Greek and Roman legends of Titans as fantasy created by writers who wished to glorify the birth of their cultures as something unique.

The following chapters make it clear that large flesh-and-blood humanoids are an integral part of the human evolutionary trajectory on planet Earth. Based on the ancient texts mentioned above, one can reasonably postulate that "giants" were a transitional genetic link between nonhumans and some subspecies of *Homo sapiens*.

To place Chouinard's important contribution within the "bigger picture" of human evolution, I propose an up-to-date, twenty-first-century view of our origins and the sweep of human history. This history includes what I call the "advanced being intervention theory" (ABIT). ABIT postulates an "intervention" of human history by beings with physical, technological, social, and psychological levels of development advanced far beyond our human abilities.

Historical accounts from all cultures describe beings who came from the skies or the waters, or even from other dimensions. Some were very much like humans, while others had animal or other forms never before seen on Earth. For these reasons they were called *devas* in Sanskrit, which means "beings from the skies or heavens." After they ceased public contact with humans, humans called them "gods" and began to worship them mentally, rather than actually bowing before a more powerful physical ruler. Due to the many different names given such beings, I use the generic term *advanced beings* or ABs. In my view, the giants discussed in this book are not ABs, but, like humans, they are hybrids between Earth-seeded species and more advanced species from other locations in our universe. However, they are an important part of the human development story on Earth.

The ABIT is supported by evidence in plain sight—but wrongly identified—in hundreds of books and thousands of academic papers available in brick-and-mortar libraries as well as online. Many describe a time when ABs from the skies descended to Earth. Most describe these ABs as fighting among themselves even as they became involved in the development of humans and their cultures. This involvement included genetic input in Earth species, but ABs also provided us with valuable assistance.

For example, the *Enûma Eliš,* the Babylonian creation myth, identifies ABs Apsu and Tiamat. Chinese myths say AB P'an Ku instructed early humans about the universe. An Apache account claims AB Hactein created human beings. Similar themes are found among artifacts in Egypt, India, Japan, and practically every other culture on the globe.

Many Sumerian, Hindu, and Hebrew texts report human interactions with advanced beings. These include the Dead Sea Scrolls, Nag Hammadi library, and Gnostic Gospels. An excellent analysis prepared by my colleague Roger Voss illustrates the quality of such information found in the oldest publicly available version of the Paleo-Hebrew Torah. Voss shows that just over two thousand years ago, Hebrew scribes still acknowledged advanced beings. For instance, Deuteronomy 10:17 states, "For Yahweh your God—He is God of the Elohim, and Lord of the lords; God, the great, the mighty, and the fearful." The names Yahweh, Lord, lords, God, and Elohim all refer to real-life ABs in both singular and plural forms. Later versions of Hebrew texts were redacted to distort these facts.

PHYSICAL EVIDENCE

Many people who are open to Chouinard's "race of giants hypothesis" believe that all the evidence comes from texts like those described above. We know that written documents are often difficult to interpret or can be edited to suggest whatever a person desires. However, the above texts have internally consistent, plausible accounts corroborated by physical artifacts.

As an example, a collection of fossilized humanoid teeth (dating to 100,000 BP) that indicate a larger bone architecture (9.5 feet tall) than *Homo sapiens sapiens* has captured the attention of open-minded scientists. Evidence points to the time period when the fossil record and DNA projections suggest *Homo sapiens sapiens* appeared. This research suggests that the giants may be the progeny of crossbreeding between ABs and the Earth genus *Homo*. This mixing of genes may have occurred "naturally" through sexual intercourse or, considering the technologically advanced capabilities of the ABs, even through genetic engineering (in vivo and in vitro gene-splicing of AB characteristics into *Homo* host cells). This correlation gives credence to biblical accounts of human-giant interactions.

There are numerous examples of contacts between humans and "giants" from prehistoric times into the modern era, including: mummies of Caucasoid humans in western China, measuring 6.5 feet in length and dating to 7000 BP; male and female mummies and skeletons of larger stature discovered in Nevada, found among artifacts dating to 10,000 BP; and sixteenth-century Spanish ship logs detailing the capture and death of 10-foot-tall humanoids.

Stories from many cultures assert that their ancestors received their language or alphabet from gods. For instance, Egyptians claim the

AB Thoth was the author of their language, and Hindus credit their Sanskrit alphabet to the AB Saraswati. Given new genetic discoveries, the AB gift of alphabets and language may have involved a genetic upgrade. The FOXP2 gene, which appeared in human form about one hundred thousand years ago, gave *Homo sapiens* control over muscles of the mouth and throat. Its appearance coincides with the leap from *Homo sapiens* to *Homo sapiens sapiens.* Insertion of this gene could explain how ABs gave giants and humans language skills beyond other hominids.

The following paragraphs connect various threads of evidence that corroborates the evolving ABIT and offer a more complex version of human history.

CORRECTING THE HUMAN STORY

Let's return to an idea introduced in the first paragraph, that most people do not know that much of what they are taught in school or college is outdated or false. In some cases, information is kept from the public because it challenges established institutions. In others, new discoveries are sidelined by stodgy procedures that delay the testing of new evidence. The more serious, historical problem, however, is the censorship and rewriting of history by elites desiring political, social, and psychological control of others. In this situation, suppression is the result of deliberate manipulation of both historical and newly discovered evidence. Consider the following.

The conventional time line of physical evolution contains many gaps in evidence. These gaps are ignored because of a tendency among academics to push aside evidence that does not support cherished theories. For instance, unexplained gaps in the fossil record are papered over with terms like *punctuated equilibrium.* Those two words mean that major shifts in evolution can't be explained by the regular slow, gradual rates of evolution. Therefore, the well-documented theory of cell-by-cell mutations—necessary for natural evolution—can't explain the gaps. Instead of being a fanciful concept, AB intervention, in my opinion, best explains these otherwise inexplicable leaps to new species. After all, humans now manipulate animal DNA, perhaps in the same way that ABs engineered modern humans through gene-splicing.

While the cover-up of genetic history is serious, the distortion of our social evolution has even more significant implications for the future. It may be interesting to learn that our bodies contain alien genes, but it is even more important to understand how ABs have influenced our intellectual and psychological development. We need to know what roles they played—and still play, as a matter of fact—in wars, technology, social unrest, and knowledge restriction.

The large majority of humans believe they and all other life-forms were directly created by a distant divine god, or gods. They consider their religious texts to be direct communication from that sacred source. This belief system has kept humans from assuming responsibility for the future of this planet and our species. It also supports attacks on those who believe differently.

The new understanding of history in this book and similar publications will make it possible for humans to rid themselves of guilt and the fear of divine retribution. The prevailing notion of an ultimate creator has kept us from realizing our true potential. Supernaturalism chains us to a very limited and inaccurate understanding of other realms and our interaction with them.

The following section details a brief case explaining why we need books like Chouinard's to help us gain a more realistic understanding of our genetic past, our social evolution, and the morphing of physical AB encounters into a supernaturalistic cosmology. We need a new way to think about what we are and how we fit into a multibeing, multidimensional universe.

DISCOVERING THE EVIDENCE

An updated story of humans on planet Earth is emerging from research that supports the AB intervention theory. However, our current knowledge is only a fragment of what will eventually be known. People who claim to have figured out all the unknowns are egoists with no desire for truth.

The first big gap in knowledge is when and how life began on this planet. The planet's birth is estimated to have happened about 4.5 billion years ago. Most scientists estimate the first single cells arose 3.8 billion years ago. However, many details concerning these events are unknown. Without access to records lost under molten rock, in the deep sea, and under shifting continental plates, such estimates are speculative.

The same problem arises with any effort to define the Earth's evolutionary tree. The ages of small organisms, plants, and animals are based on the rates of radioactive decay in certain isotopes or in the rock layers in which they are found. Carbon-14 dating is useful only for specimens less than fifty thousand years old. Thus, the evolutionary time line contains gaps that await new technologies to fill in the blanks.

With these caveats, I sketch out below a plausible time line of human history based on the work of Pat Chouinard and others. Drawing on their research and some of my own, we can construct a skeletal theory—leaving it open to new discoveries in science and history—of how humans reached a population of more than seven billion souls.

About six million years ago, a variety of hominids existed on Earth, in the view of most scientists. These creatures apparently changed at a gradual rate of evolution. It is likely that by 2.5 million BP the genus *Homo* appeared. Some of them evolved into *Homo erectus* types about 2 million BP. These *erectus* types had humanlike bodies and appear to be our direct Earth ancestors.

However, we must consider the possibility that extraplanetary scientists seeded life on Earth in its early geophysical conditions. Or, perhaps they simply took advantage of early species and experimented with them over time. Either way, the evidence suggests that ABs very likely played a role in creating modern species.

Between 300,000 and 200,000 BP, the slowly evolving *erectus* types—with tool-making and social skills—began to be replaced in an inexplicably short period of time by *Homo sapiens* arising in Africa. Ancient texts reviewed by Zecharia Sitchin and others, including myself, hold sufficient corroborative evidence to make the case that ABs could have been involved in this "leap" in the evolutionary time line.

About 100,000 BP, we have another "leap" over a "gap" in the fossil record. At that point, an even greater modification in the *sapiens* genome occurred, producing *Homo sapiens sapiens*. Fifty thousand years later, a diaspora of these modern humans took place. As they traveled across continents, they likely interbred with contemporary descendants of *erectus* types in different locations.

These *erectus-sapiens* matings may have produced Neanderthals and Denisovans. The former have been tentatively placed in Europe and the latter in East Asia. They appeared in our fossil record forty thousand years ago or earlier. That modern *Homo sapiens sapiens* interbred with these subspecies is validated by the discovery of their DNA in modern humans. Such common genes among all these groups may suggest that AB genes provide internal links among humanoids from the beginning.

During the *sapiens sapiens* diaspora described above and 11,500 BP (the date of the biblical flood, a global cataclysm), self-described, AB-assisted human communities arose on various parts of the planet. Legends of Lemuria, Atlantis, and other sites noted for highly developed civilizations fit into that time frame.

This is the first period of apparent miscegenation (not genetic manipulation) between "the gods" and *sapiens,* resulting in AB-human hybrids. A variety of AB-human genotypes were produced, a result of different kinds of ABs having intercourse with humans. These hybrids may include some of the "giants of old" discussed in this book among the subspecies of the general category we call *Homo sapiens.*

At the same time, aboriginal *sapiens sapiens* kept to themselves in Africa and several more isolated locations. Their offspring, who did not interbreed with descendants of independent *erectus-sapiens* types, generally had a smaller body type. These include various groups of pygmies, like the so-called "hobbits" discovered in Indonesia in 2003, dated to at least 18,000 BP.

These aboriginals who escaped the later widespread miscegenation between ABs and *Homo sapiens sapiens* were able to maintain cultures that produced more objective views of the AB gods. Their legends of "the gods" were formed at a distance, in contrast to biblical and other texts describing intimate, ongoing AB-human relations.

Readers must keep in mind that the evidence for the above dates is sparse. This means that these descriptions of human history from 250,000 to 12,000 years ago are based on inferences from many different sources. Fortunately, recent fossil and genetic analyses support the idea of AB intervention during that period.

As you progress through the pages of this book, you will find references to the "sky people" or extraterrestrials, in many of the accounts. Keep the ideas of my foreword in mind as you read these myths and stories, and you may begin to see how credible the idea of AB intervention really is.

PARTIAL FOSSIL RECORD

The fossil record as we currently know it shows that our hominid ancestors slowly evolved over six million years. They coped with harsh conditions with little genetic mutation. Yet, between three hundred thousand and two hundred thousand years ago, a nimble and intelligent new species, *Homo sapiens,* appeared in Africa outside the *erectus* pace of genetic mutation.

After about one hundred thousand years or so, another anomalous gap occurred in the genetic evolution of the *Homo* genus. From that period *Homo sapiens sapiens* fossils can be found in Africa and beyond. With complex language and tools, these modern humans demonstrated greater mental skills with no increase in brain capacity.

Multiple sites illustrate this rapid divergence. *Erectus*-type stone hand axes and other tools that date to 700,000 BP were found in South Africa and on Crete (an island separated from Africa for millions of years). Similar simple tools were still in use 130,000 years ago, while *Homo sapiens sapiens* had advanced to building ships and sailing them along far-ranging seafaring routes.

This fossil record is consistent with Sumern and Hebrew texts that describe AB upgrades of humans. The rabbinical scribes at the time of the Babylonian exile (the sixth century BCE) still accepted the historical claims that the Elohim (ABs) had raised humans above the other animals on Earth. Genesis 1:26 "let them have dominion over (all animals and the earth)."

INDIRECT DNA CORROBORATION

The genetic changes producing *Homo sapiens* occurred in a very short period rather than over hundreds of thousands or millions of years. This gap in human evolution requires an extraordinary explanation. External genetic manipulation could have created a new species such as *Homo sapiens*. Genesis 1:26 offers evidence of just that: "the Elohim said, Let us make man in our Image."

No male Y-chromosome analysis to date places an *Adam* coexistent with *Eve*. The Genesis texts suggest the *Adam* event occurred prior to *Eve*. If male AB colonists provided Y chromosomes that morphed *erectus* types into *Homo sapiens,* this order makes sense. The so-called *Eve* creation event could have been after the *Adam* event if its AB-human genes were then spliced, either in vivo or in vitro, into host cells of only a few female *Homo sapiens.*

From the analysis of mitochondrial DNA, researchers now believe that *Homo sapiens sapiens* came from only a few females in Africa between one hundred thousand and two hundred thousand years ago. This dating of the *Eve* event is consistent with the fossil record and the Annunaki/human time line first publicized by Sitchin. It also precedes the date (between 100,000 and 50,000 BP) that has been validated for *Homo sapiens sapiens'* arrival in Europe and Central Asia.

Other genetic events also have links with our hypothetical story line. The advent of various blood-type genes also coincides with periods of AB involvement in human history since the Cataclysm. Survivors of Noah's Ark in the Turkic-Mesopotamian region have a higher-than-average type B percentage than the people living in adjacent areas, who are mainly type O. Other blood types' appearances coincide with reported AB interventions.

The first phase in AB intervention in hominid development was impersonal, technical gene-splicing. But, as *Homo sapiens* quickly evolved physically and mentally, their interactions with ABs became more personal, leading to *Homo sapiens sapiens.*

Cohabitation between AB colonizers and humans occurred during both the pre- and post-Cataclysm eras. Humans who labored for the ABs or became members of their households obviously learned a lot from them. But, the phase known as Exile from Eden is a turning point. Humans lost direct access to AB knowledge and technologies.

AFTER THE GLOBAL CATACLYSM

After 11,500 BP, we move from fragmented evidence of our early history to a fairly good sample of documentation that still exists. These sources need only be looked at through a new set of lenses (ancient astronaut and AB intervention theories). By 11,500 BP, advanced civilizations around the globe had been destroyed, leaving only small groups of survivors who had lost their technologies, habitats, and social cohesion.

Accounts from around the world describe how ABs landed back on Earth after the volcanic explosions, nuclear-winter-type darkness, earthquakes, regional floods, mountain upheavals, loss of species, and devastation of human cultures. Hebrew, Babylonian, and other regional texts describe assistance from ABs following a great flood or deluge, including advice on crops and animal husbandry.

Lucky human survivors received technical assistance in several key locations around the globe, including Mesopotamia, western China, India, the Andes, and possibly others. In less than two thousand years, sophisticated cultures blossomed with AB technical assistance at several locations. Pre-Cataclysm human memories that survived were fragmented and often vague but included recollections of pre-Cataclysm AB involvement with humans. Some of these memories hint of high civilizations such as Lemuria or Atlantis, or special places like Eden or Shambhala.

The reader will note that this history is inconsistent with what we are taught in school. Academics assume that ten thousand years ago (after the abrupt, cataclysmic ending of the Ice Age), humans had evolved only to the "caveman" stage. But for decades now, each year brings increasing discoveries of unexpectedly sophisticated human activities quickly after the Cataclysm. Fortunately, we also still have bits of the Atlantean and complementing memories that can be verified with research, as discussed in this book.

HOW DOES ATLANTIS FIT?

Does the story of Atlantis fit into the time line described above? Some writers using extradimensional sources have proposed the Atlantean civilization enjoyed a long history, perhaps almost extending one hundred thousand years. As squishy as such a claim may be, it is interesting that the above evidence points to *Homo sapiens sapiens* about that time. If correct, it would also correlate with other so-called Atlantean "memories."

One belief is that the "gods" at the beginning of Atlantean history were super beings who directly ruled humans. The founder of Atlantis, Poseidon, was alleged to be one of them. Thus, his ten direct offspring (the oldest being Atlas) with the human Cleito were hybrids who were later known as the rulers of Atlantis. These ideas are consistent with AB interventions in the fossil and DNA record described earlier, including evidence of giants.

Other subjective material suggests these AB-hybrid rulers made possible the ascent of the first utopian civilization among humans. While initially ruled by these demigods, the human citizens were largely independent and involved in self-government. Immigrants from Atlantis may have taken this ideal to other humans before the sinking of its final remnants during the Cataclysm. Indian, European, Middle Eastern, and American legends still carry accounts of such utopian practices.

However, fragmented accounts also include descriptions of conflict among Poseidon's siblings and cohorts. Their internecine AB wars are also consistent with worldwide origin myths, including those depicted in the Hebrew Bible.

Of course, pre-Cataclysm cultures were decimated when civilizations everywhere suffered almost a total loss of their populations, structures, and technologies. However, images of Atlantis survived in the minds of survivors, and were passed on to the Egyptians, and then to the Greeks. They included tales of the giants described later in this book.

With the loss of most of the Atlantean civilization, except for a few escapees who scattered across India, Europe, North Africa, and parts of the Americas, the human story becomes one of new AB efforts to revive human communities. But those efforts were a double-edged sword—not unlike the results of advanced European nations colonizing indigenous cultures around the world over the past five hundred years.

POST-ATLANTEAN CIVILIZATION

The post-Cataclysm stories, as in Noah's tale, describe AB assistance that helped humans rebuild. The downside was a return of AB colonial rule, as hinted at in the Garden of Eden story. Just as in modern European colonies, the revival of human culture did not escape the "subjugation/self-deprecation syndrome" imposed by the ABs.

Several survival accounts (Sumerian, Hebrew, Sanskrit, and African) describe conflicts among the "gods" affecting their human tribes. This off-planet discord caused the AB colonizers to quit their overt Earth rule before 4000 BP. They left humans to their own devices or under kings or queens with direct AB bloodlines. Lists of Egyptian rulers track this shift: ABs gave way to fifth-millennium hybrid kings, followed by the pharaohs, who imitated and claimed to be descendants of AB gods.

The first semi-AB kings and priests turned their regencies into sects to manipulate people into continuing worship of their absentee AB godparents. These cults stifled intellectual and social progress, and drove modern human civilization into its first Dark Ages. Squabbling kings and priests perpetuated religious wars humans fought under the flags of their AB overlords for millennia.

Pyramids or ziggurats were built (or rebuilt) after the Cataclysm, when ABs rendered technical assistance to human survivors. During that period, the AB custom of intercourse with humans resumed. Biblical accounts note that AB-human mating created a bloodline of hybrid giants active as late as King David's rule, three thousand years ago.

The AB domestic structures described in the previous paragraph deteriorated after the overt withdrawal of ABs from human societies. By the fifth century BCE (ABs had been absent for a millennium or more), Greek historian Herodotus, describing the cradle of Western Civilization, reported the ziggurats had fallen into ruin.

As centuries passed without a return of the ABs, the weakening bloodlines began to lose their spell over their subjects. To continue control over new generations, loyal priests began to reshape the historical facts about ABs into supernatural terms. Inventing the idea of a supernatural heaven accessible only through them gave the priests an advantage over the masses. Cult leaders, including Roman popes, declared only they had a divine channel to receive messages from the departed AB gods.

In this manner, "supernatural religions" were created to replace the AB-based cults. This sleight-of-hand, shifting the human focus from real ABs to unreal gods, kept humans under the psychological sway of authoritarian leaders with their own political agendas. The result was centuries of sectarian warfare, crusades, torture, inquisitions, and mind-control techniques developed by supernaturalistic theocrats.

For the last two millennia humans have struggled between this supernatural-based hypnotic state and our natural, biological impulse to realize our own potential. With humans mired in emotional stagnation largely of human creation, many of us are now (with input from enlightened ABs) trying to reveal the real story behind the cover-up.

In conclusion, I believe evidence compels us to accept being a hybrid species. As described above, this was well known by humans at the dawn of modern history. The knowledge was then distorted by kings and priests who took advantage of less aware humans, psychologically manipulating them to serve their economic and political agendas.

Chouinard's valuable research into AB-human interbreeding, resulting in different types of humanoids, will fill in significant gaps in human history.

An interdisciplinary cosmologist and independent scholar, PAUL VON WARD is internationally known for the hypothesis of advanced being intervention in human development; his theory of natural spirituality in an evolving, self-learning universe; and research on the survival of a personal soul genome. His current books on these topics are *We've Never Been Alone, Our Solarian Legacy,* and *The Soul Genome*. Paul's academic background (Florida State, Harvard, and the University of Southern California, among others); his military, diplomatic, and international executive career; and his research on five continents keep his provocative publications grounded in emerging science and credible human experience.

The Giant Phenomenon and Black Holes of Scientific Endeavor

Who could forget the final scene of *Raiders of the Lost Ark* in which a crated "Ark of the Covenant" is wheeled into a massive top-secret warehouse? The final seconds of the movie are filled with rows of thousands of neatly stacked crates, all allegedly containing anomalous finds that the government sought to keep hidden from the public eye—out of sight, out of mind. Only in the conclusion to the Indiana Jones saga, *Indiana Jones and the Kingdom of the Crystal Skull,* do we get a glimpse of where the warehouse of forbidden items was actually located: at a restricted government facility in the Desert Southwest, probably Area 51.*

Of course, we know this was merely an invention of Hollywood, nothing more. Right? No, not really, for sadly enough there really are black holes of scientific endeavor where startling new discoveries have

---

*Area 51 is a remote part of Edwards Air Force Base in Nevada, which is used for top-secret experiments by the U.S. Air Force, acting in conjunction with the CIA.

been banished, to never again see the light of day. These knowledge pits are the point of no return for many findings considered to be too radical to fit into the established paradigm; they are suppressed by institutions intent on maintaining the status quo.

A perfect example of this type of suppression occurred in 1962, when an archaeological dig in Mexico, at Hueyatlaco, a Paleo-Indian site 121 kilometers southeast of Mexico City, yielded discoveries that did not fit within the accepted time line. In 1962, Mexican archaeologist Juan Armenta Camacho and American archaeologist Cynthia Irwin-Williams unearthed sophisticated stone tools dating to 250,000 BP, which upended traditional theories about the cultural development of early humans. Startled by the anomalous nature of what they discovered, these two archaeologists attempted to suppress the findings. In 1966, graduate student Virginia Steen-McIntyre joined their dig and, unlike the other two archaeologists, was very outspoken about discussing and attempting to publish the earth-shattering news; however, she was to face tremendous roadblocks in her efforts. Her statements were ridiculed—it was as though she were claiming that Bigfoot lived in the White House! She was promptly fired from her position as geologist and field archaeologist and stripped of her prestige as a respected member of the academic community. Furthermore, never again was she able to get a job in her beloved field of archaeology or any legitimate position as a mainstream geologist (Gallegos 2009, 10).

Steen-McIntyre had this to say about the matter in a letter she wrote to Estella Leopold, the associate editor of *Quaternary Research:*

> The problem as I see it is much bigger than Hueyatlaco. It concerns the manipulation of scientific thought through the suppression of "Enigmatic Data," data that challenges the prevailing mode of thinking. Hueyatlaco certainly does that! Not being an anthropologist, I didn't realize the full significance of our dates back in 1973, nor how deeply woven into our thought the current theory

of human evolution had become. Our work at Hueyatlaco has been rejected by most archaeologists because it contradicts that theory, period. (gdub 2012)

Another victim of this knowledge filter is Polish scholar Immanuel Velikovsky. Although the late, great Carl Sagan readily identified himself with what my friend John Anthony West calls the priesthood of science, Sagan made a heroic appeal on behalf of Velikovsky, who is best known for his book *Worlds in Collision,* published in 1950. Velikovsky's theories included the idea that Venus was actually an anomaly generated in the Jovian system* (Sagan 1980, 90–91). Velikovsky maintained that the planet, or comet as he called it, left the gravitational influence of Jupiter and entered the inner solar system approximately 3500 BCE. During two close encounters with Earth in 1450 BCE, the direction of Earth's rotation was altered radically (Alexander 2005, 21–24).

According to Velikovsky, Earth's rotation then reverted to its original direction on its next pass through the orbit of the inner solar system. In the second and final confrontation with Earth, the comet caused substantial volcanism, floods, and even the parting of the Red Sea as described in the Book of Exodus. Following this phase of its journey, it settled into its current orbit and became the planet Venus as we know it today.[†]

Sagan reported that the academic community attempted to suppress Velikovsky's ideas about Venus, and he (Sagan) condemned these actions. Velikovsky was forbidden from speaking at universities and publishing his ideas in scientific journals, and newspapers and other media were dissuaded from releasing updates on his research. "Science," concluded Sagan, "is generated by and devoted to free inquiry; the idea

---

*The Jovian system refers to the planet Jupiter as well as its moons, its Trojan asteroids, and its magnetosphere.
†Mars also passed dangerously close to Earth between 776 and 687 BCE, prompting Earth's axis to oscillate by ten degrees (Alexander 2005, 21–24).

that any hypothesis, no matter how strange, deserves to be considered on its merits. The suppression of uncomfortable ideas may be common in religion and politics, but it is not the path to knowledge; it has no place in the endeavor of science" (1980, 90–91).

Against this broader backdrop of systemic scientific suppression we have the fields of modern-day archaeology and anthropology, whose gatekeepers have severely curtailed the potentialities of much current comprehensive scholarly research that seeks to explore the anomalous and fascinating question of whether giants were part of hominid evolution on Earth. Given that this is the case, my work here is to provide evidence that the race of giants theory is a true one. In so doing, I call upon and cite innumerable accounts in the written record that are difficult to disprove. Here is but a sampling of what awaits you in the pages of this book.

In referencing the possibility of giants in ancient North America, the late Native American author, historian, and theologian Vine Deloria wrote:

The first hint we had about the possible existence of an actual race of tall, strong, and intellectually sophisticated people, was in researching old township and county records. Many of these were quoting from old diaries and letters that were combined, for posterity, in the 1800s, from diaries going back to the 1700s. Some of these old county and regional history books contain real gems because the people were not subjected to a rigid indoctrination about evolution and were astonished about what they found and honestly reported it. ("Holocaust of Giants")

The building up of infrastructure in the mid-1800s in the United States—the construction of a road system, the breaking of new ground for the construction of homes, and the building of key government and community buildings—revealed hundreds of human skeletons of gigantic stature. The following account originated around the year 1800 in Ohio:

> There were mounds situated in the eastern part of the village of Conneaut and an extensive burying-ground near the Presbyterian church, which appear to have had no connection with the burying-places of the Indians. Among the human bones founds in the mounds were some belonging to men of gigantic structure. Some of the skulls were of sufficient capacity to admit the head of an ordinary man, and jaw bones that might have been fitted on over the face with equal facility; the other bones were proportionately large. The burial-ground referred to contained about four acres, and with the exception of a slight angle in conformity with the natural contour of the ground was in the form of an oblong square. It appeared to have been accurately surveyed into lots running from north to south, and exhibited all the order and propriety of arrangement deemed necessary to constitute Christian burial. ("Holocaust of Giants")

And we have this account in an article entitled "Mysterious Giant Human Skeleton Discovered in Saudi Arabia," which was recently published on numerous sites on the Internet. The author of the article, who elected to remain anonymous, writes:

> Recent gas exploration activity in the southeast region of the Arabian Desert uncovered the skeletal remains of a human of phenomenal size. The region of the Arabian Desert is called the Empty Quarter, or in Arabic, "Rab-Ul-Khalee." The Aramco Exploration team made the discovery. As God states in the Qu'ran, He had created people of phenomenal size the likes of which He has not created since. These were the people of Aad where Prophet Hud was sent. They were very tall, big, and very powerful, such that they could put their arms around a tree trunk and uproot it. After these people,

who were given all the power, turned against God and the Prophet and transgressed beyond all boundaries set by God. As a result they were destroyed. Ulema's [sic] of Saudi Arabia believe these to be the remains of the people of Aad. Saudi Military has secured the whole area and no one is allowed to enter except the Aramco personnel. It has been kept in secrecy, but a military helicopter took some pictures from the air and one of the pictures leaked out into the Internet in Saudi Arabia. ("Mysterious")

Regardless of the evidence, institutions such as the Smithsonian, the U.S. government, and the majority of American universities have not only systematically discouraged investigation into reports or hard physical evidence of ancient peoples of gigantic stature, they have furtively buried the evidence. Why? The discovery of a race of giants is a threat to the established order. Disclosure would not only mean an end to the prevailing paradigm, but would also completely alter our worldview, given that an assumption about the validity of giants is necessarily inclusive of the idea that intelligent life on other planets is, in fact, a stark reality that we must face—whether we like it or not.

This book presents the historical, mythological, and archaeological evidence for "the race of giants" hypothesis. In this, it attempts to lay the foundation of several new theories, including the role giants played in human evolution. I hope you enjoy reading it as much as I did researching and writing it.

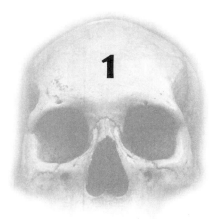

Giants and Mythology

A Global Story

We must not remind them that giants walk the earth.
Frank Miller, *Batman: The Dark Knight Returns*, 1987

Even though human memory fails to penetrate the true mysteries of our remote past, mythology provides us with a framework by which we can glean a semblance of humanity's origins in prehistory and come to an understanding of who we are as a species. The many myths of giants, gods, and other advanced beings whose power supposedly once ruled this planet today remain the strongest nonarchaeological evidence we have to support the idea that a race of giants once peopled the Earth.

In this chapter we will explore many of these myths, which are more than nebulous accounts concocted by unsophisticated humans—much more than metaphors or stories bearing symbolic or religious significance. They are what survive of our history prior to the great age of cataclysms, which destroyed the global civilization and changed humanity and this planet for the subsequent eight millennia. Now, for the first time, the truth about giants and our past is finally coming to light.

SEMANTIC DERIVATION OF THE TERM *GIANT*

In our remote past, giants were worshipped as gods. Indeed, almost all of the gods and goddesses of antiquity were of gigantic stature. Why is this so? Part of the answer may be found in an examination of the semantics involved: The roots of the word *god* can be traced back to the Germanic word *Gott,* and prior to the introduction of this particular title, there existed the Latin *deus* and the Greek *theos.* In ancient times, even in the Hebrew tradition, it was widely known that these words—those signifying a power greater than oneself—applied not to a single omnipotent being but rather "beings from the sky" (always denoted in the plural). In the annals and chronicles of ancient times, both gods and giants have been categorized as "advanced beings" or "sky gods." This is a very interesting point in and of itself, but it also raises an important question: What difference, if any, exists between gods and giants?

Who were these giants described in ancient times? Were they mere fantasies, or do they represent a very real, very tangible link to our prehistoric ancestors? Mainstream science teaches us that creatures such as giants, ogres, and other monstrous beings are merely mythical icons from our remote past and have no basis in reality. Our ancestors, terrified of a world they did not understand and could not control, devised these myths to bring order and predictability to a chaotic, primeval world. Such are the conclusions of academia, but these simplistic views of an ignorant and credulous human race is in its final death throes. Through a study of ancient mythology, combined with advances in archaeology and technology, we are coming to understand that the ancients were actually highly advanced and may have possessed technologies comparable to or even surpassing our own. They were, for example, excellent record keepers, and had a significant knowledge of astronomy, medicine, and engineering. Thus we ought to take seriously their seemingly extraordinary tales of Titans, frost giants, and Cyclopes.

THE FEATS AND WISDOM OF THE ANCIENTS

In order to show that the giants of antiquity were not the product of an unsophisticated imagination, it is necessary to first establish as fact the feats and wisdom of the ancients. This inevitably leads into to a discussion of their premodern technological achievements, some far more advanced than those of today. Once their sophistication has been demonstrated, we can more objectively address the issue of the existence of giants.

What we have found is that the civilizations of the ancient world were far more advanced than many archaeologists are prepared to admit. A deceptively small device found in 1900 on the island of Antikythera, twenty-five miles northwest of Crete, lends credence to this assertion. Retrieved from the submerged wreckage of a Greek galley by fishermen and sponge divers, the device was actually a working computer, intricately devised not by Apple or Dell, but by the Greeks during Hellenistic times (circa 323–146 BCE). David Childress, author of *Technology of the Gods* (2000), rightfully boasts of its discovery as being "tantamount to finding a jet airplane in the tomb of King Tut."

Hints of other technological feats from antiquity have survived into the twenty-first century as well. For example, texts and detailed drawings of flying craft called *vimāna* in the Sanskrit writings of India give us at least some indication that in the remote past, someone—or something—flew the skies above Earth.

Let's assume for the moment that the ancient traditions of the gods imparting knowledge and wisdom to the early human race are not mere fantasy, but based on eyewitness accounts of actual events. This, then, would not be a misinterpreted record of an ancient alien visitation, but a direct account of an early race of giants passing on what it had learned from the gods to humans in a form of succession, passing the torch to another generation of ancient Terrans, or earthborn beings.

One of the many tribes of humanity that were passed the torch of civilization very early on from the primeval giants of old were the Chinese. Confucius records that in China, during the reign of the Five Monarchs, from 2852 to 2206 BCE, "flying carriages" existed in that country. However, it is difficult to ascertain the full extent of the technological wonders the ancient Chinese may have possessed because, prior to his death circa 210–209 BCE, Emperor Chin Shih Huang Ti ordered the burning of hundreds of thousands of books, including all those in the royal libraries (Childress 2000). A few lucky tomes, however, escaped the wrath of the imperial torches, and from them a few accounts of advanced technology possessed by the ancient Chinese have survived to this very day.

The ancient Chinese, in addition to the invention of flying craft and military technology, also developed practical innovations for mass consumption. An individual named Bi Sheng introduced the technology of movable type in 1045 CE, more than four centuries before the printing of the first Gutenberg Bible. And to resist earthquakes, quite common in China, the Chinese are rumored to have invented the first earthquake-resistant houses. Moreover, around 725 CE two Chinese inventors are credited with developing the first mechanical clock. In addition, gunpowder was common to the Chinese, which they employed beginning in the ninth century or earlier. Gunpowder was used for fireworks and as a means to frighten opposing armies or to announce the coming of an invading force rather than as a weapon.

According to Childress:

The Chinese have always had great scope and vision regarding their projects; not only was the Great Wall a colossal endeavor, but the

Grand Canal of China, which connects the Yellow River with the Yangtze, is twenty times longer than the Panama Canal—yet the Chinese constructed it without modern equipment starting over 1,300 years ago! There are other mammoth projects that are still unknown or waiting to be discovered, such as the largest pyramid in the world, near Xian. Even the Chinese version of the typewriter, called the Hoang typewriter, has 5,700 characters on a keyboard two feet wide and seventeen inches high! (Childress 1998, 396)

Chinese armies also employed the use of poison gas more than 2,500 years before it was invented and used by the West in World War I. They also developed cast iron in the fourth century BCE, more than 1,700 years before it was first used by Europeans, and created steel from cast iron in the second century BCE—more than 2,000 years before Westerners manufactured it.

How is it that the Chinese were so technologically advanced at such an early stage of their culture's development? Renowned British scientist, historian, and sinologist Joseph Needham of Cambridge University echoes this very question when he writes (with regard to the splendor of early Chinese inventions): "First, why should they have been so far in advance of other civilizations; and second, why aren't they now centuries ahead of the rest of the world?" (Childress 1998, 397) David Childress implies that the answer lies in inherited knowledge from an older civilization. "Its discoveries," writes Childress, "like ours, are just the re-discovery of ancient technology from the roller-coaster ride of history" (Childress 1998, 397).

I posit that this was because Chinese civilization may have been jump-started by an extramundane source during the time when the primeval giants passed on knowledge to the chosen people of the new era. As you will see, we will argue for this theory throughout the book, as it is one of the foundational tenets of our research.

GIANTS AS PART OF OUR COLLECTIVE UNCONSCIOUS

Since they first walked the Earth eons ago, giants have become a part of our collective unconscious, a terrifying Jungian archetype that captivates the imagination. They form the cornerstone of the myths, legends, and traditions of almost every culture on Earth, and in many cases, these narratives have remained unchanged for millennia. Such myths often depict a civilization ruled by giants that is destroyed by a global deluge and eventually forgotten.

These myths and legends help us to decode the secrets of that forgotten chapter in human history. Indeed, these gigantic inhabitants of our imagination are not mere figments, but rather the cultural phantom "residue" from our past experiences as a species. They are, in fact, imprints or echoes of a remote but very real Dark Age that we have mostly long since forgotten—until now. As with all mythological accounts, they are but blurred images of a far more profound reality.

Let's look at some specific examples of giants mentioned in the myths and legends of the world, beginning with the Inca civilization.

- Inca myth describes the *Ayar-aucca* race, which includes four twin giants who hold up the sky. In this myth (as in many others like it) the human race becomes unruly and ungrateful. Angered by this, the four giants agree to let the sky tumble down and crash into the sea. The result is a global flood that obliterates much of humankind (Joseph 2005). (The idea of the sky crashing to Earth and destroying virtually all of civilization resonates with Plato's Atlantis and some of the more recent speculation regarding its demise. Some theories suggest that a comet or asteroid may have impacted Earth sometime during our remote history, causing the destruction of these ancient and advanced cultures.)
- In Irish mythology, we learn of the *Formorach,* a giant sea people. Their leader, Balor, guides them to the shores of Ireland follow-

ing the Great Flood. They then become the native inhabitants of that island. While some scholars locate the Formorach's point of origin in Spain or North Africa, others claim that the original homeland of these pre-Celtic giants was Atlantis, thought to have been located two hundred miles west of Gibraltar (Joseph 2005).

- The Giant's Causeway in Northern Ireland is also linked to giants in that its natural geologic formations consist of massive basalt columns that were claimed to have been the work of the giants.

- In the third millennium BCE, the *Hurrians* were the dominant race of Anatolia. The Hittites, who conquered the Hurrians around 2000 BCE, absorbed many of their religious beliefs and mythological traditions, including the myth of Alalu, the first king of heaven—a giant god who thrived on a mountainous island situated in the Western Ocean, which was often referred to as the sea of the setting sun. (The Western Ocean was an earlier name for the Atlantic Ocean.) Author and historian Frank Joseph believes that this tradition of giant gods and the island in the Atlantic is a Hurrian memory of the mountainous island of Atlantis. Alalu's son was the mighty Kumarbi, the mythic personification of the Atlantic Ocean and the Hurrian equivalent of the Greek Titan Kronos. Kumarbi placed the world on his mountainous neck. In this, in addition to being the equivalent of Kronos, he also was the Anatolian equivalent of the Greek deity and Titan Atlas, the founder of the mighty Atlantean empire (Joseph 2005).

- The Kai of New Guinea recalled a race of demigods, or giants, called the *Ne-Mu*. They were said to be taller and stronger than the mortal race of today, but they were lords of the Earth before the Great Flood. They taught the Kai ancestors the fundamentals of agriculture and house construction. The Ne-Mu were wiped out during the Deluge, but their bodies were transformed into blocks of stone. "This final feature of the myth," Frank Joseph writes (2005), "betrays the Kai's reaction to megalithic structures found occasionally in New Guinea, often composed of prodigious stonework they identify with the pre-Flood Ne-Mu."

- The natives of the Fijian islands believe that their ancestral land, called Burotu, sank long ago into the Pacific Ocean. This ancestral realm was obliterated when the "heavens fell down," and fire and water melded together to produce the islands of Samoa. The survivors, known as the *Hiti,* were thought to be a race of giants: the children of Atlantis. They built a monumental arch standing almost twenty feet high (Joseph 2005).

- Arabic myth describes a race of giants known as the *Adites.* These beings are the equivalent of the Atlantean Titans of Greek mythology, and are described as superior architects and builders. Since their earliest recorded history, Arabs in the Middle East have associated all immense structures with these great giants of antiquity. (We will read more about the building and civilizing skills of ancient giants in the following chapter.)

- Bochica is a figure in the myths of the Chibcha peoples of present-day Colombia. A bearded, white-skinned giant similar to Atlas, he supports the sky on his shoulders. When the people forsake his teachings, he eventually drops the sky, causing a series of floods and conflagrations that decimate the planet. This event also destroys the giant's own home, forcing his children to flee and seek shelter elsewhere. In the end, they settle along the coast of Colombia, eventually becoming the country's native Indian inhabitants (Joseph 2005).

As you can see from this small sampling, the sheer number and variety of giant myths and legends is staggering. Indeed, they can be found in almost every culture on Earth. As stated above, many of these mythologies include beings closely related to the Titans, who supposedly once ruled Atlantis. And of course there is also the recurring narrative of a great cataclysm that destroyed a civilization sometime in the remote past. Such common themes and motifs lay the groundwork for an even broader discussion. Let's examine some additional accounts of giants now.

GIANTS IN INDIA

In the spring of 2000, in a virtually uninhabited desert region of northern India, an American team of archaeologists uncovered the ancient skeletal remains of a human being of phenomenal size. An elite team of excavators from the American government made the discovery, with support from the Indian military, which holds jurisdiction over the area.

Along with the gigantic bones, the team discovered tablets bearing ancient inscriptions. These tablets detailed a story from Indian mythology regarding the supreme god Brahma, who existed in the beginning and created the cosmos as we know it. This deity, according to the inscription, created creatures of gargantuan size in the remote past and commanded them to bring order to chaos. They soon became the rulers and guardians of humans. But they were constantly combating each other and engaging in profuse military engagements along with fits of aggression and territoriality. They eventually failed their purpose and had to be destroyed.

Some sources claim that the American team and the Indian government secretly believe that these cyclopean relics belong to the vanished race of giants that Brahma created. Following the initial excavation, the Indian government sealed off the area, allowing access only to Indian government officials and authorized representatives of the American government.

In the Sanskrit writings of India we learn of the *Daityas*, or water giants. They are mentioned in the Vishnu Purana and the Mahabharata, two of the most ancient and highly revered Hindu sacred texts. The Daityas are the offspring of Vishnu. These water giants are the East Indian equivalent of the Titans of Greek mythology, which include

Atlas and the other kings of Atlantis. These writings describe how Vishnu's mother conquers the Earth for the gods and becomes the first of the mighty Daitya. This ultimately makes her the upholder of the sky—what Frank Joseph describes as "the moral order of the cosmos"—therefore identifying her with the Greek Titan Atlas, who creates the island of Atlantis and holds the burden of the world on his shoulders (Joseph 2005).

According to the Vishnu Purana, these water giants reside in Tripura, the Triple City. This metropolis, now a sunken island, located far across the impenetrable Western Ocean (the Atlantic Ocean), echoes Plato's own descriptions of the lost civilization of Atlantis. The immortal Greek philosopher wrote that this submerged landmass was beyond the Pillars of Hercules in the middle of the Atlantic Ocean. In addition, the Triple City of the Vishnu Purana is clearly emblematic of the trident of Poseidon, the patron god of Atlantis. In a final war, both the Daitya and Tripura are destroyed, which is yet another similarity to the myth of Atlantis (Joseph 2005).

The *Rakshas* are also worthy of recognition, if only for their gruesome and diabolical reputations. Hindu belief maintains that the Rakshas were thoroughly wicked humans in previous incarnations and that their reincarnation as one of these hideous giants was punishment for past sins. According to the Ramayana, these giants were born from Brahma's foot. Other myths trace their bloodline back to the demon Pulastya or to other devils, such as Khasa, Nirriti, or Nirrita.

Rakshas are described as mean, vicious creatures, exceedingly ugly, gigantic in stature, and black as soot. Unequaled in their ferocity, they interrupted sacrifices, desecrated burial sites, harassed priests, and took possession of impressionable young humans; in fact, their crimes are too numerous to describe here in full. They were often depicted with two fangs protruding out of their mouths like vampires, with sharp, nail-like claws, prowling through the night like wandering beasts. Due to their obvious connection to the mythology of vampires, Rakshas have also been associated with the undead. Further emphasizing their venomous, beastlike persona, they were also portrayed as cannibals.

But descriptions such as these are consistent with ancient folk custom and Hindu lore. In the world of the great epics, the Ramayana and Mahabharata, the Rakshas have greater significance. According to the great epics, the Rakshas are a populous race of supernatural humanoid giants. Some Rakshas follow the path of righteousness; others have simply degenerated into evil. They have proven themselves in battle as supreme lords of war, and they are also gifted magic-users and skilled shape-shifters. They are known to gulp down the blood-drenched legs and torsos of fallen soldiers on the battlefield, and thus are employed as rank and file combat soldiers to keep them from obtaining any true prominence. But sometimes Rakshas would attain distinction and be considered heroes.

GIANTS IN ANCIENT GREEK MYTHOLOGY

The earliest known Greek deities, the Titans, ruled the primordial universe before the coming of the Olympians. (This parallels the biblical Nephilim, who ruled the Earth until their age ended, giving rise to humans.) Atlas, perhaps the most well known of the Titans, was the ruler of Atlantis and, as Frank Joseph notes in *The Atlantis Encyclopedia* (2005), the founder of astrology and astronomy. Atlas* is often depicted in illustrations as a gigantic, bearded man crouching on one knee and bearing the sphere of the heavens upon his massive shoulders. Given this, and perhaps not surprisingly, the Sanskrit word *atl* means "to support or uphold." Such imagery has come to signify the Atlanteans' stalwart dedication to celestial and planetary sciences.

The later Olympian Greeks had their own giants, the *Gigantes*—

---

*Interestingly enough, Atlas is also the name of a mountain in Asia Minor not far from the incredible ruins of Çatalhüyük, which is more than nine thousand years old, making it arguably the oldest city on Earth. It may date back to the destruction of Atlantis or may even be the first colony of its fleeing survivors (Joseph 2005).

grotesque, humanoid creatures with serpentine legs. In the myth narratives, they attempted to overthrow Zeus and the other gods of Mount Olympus, but ultimately failed. The Greek saga *The Agronautica* describes these giants in the following manner: "Their bodies have three pairs of nerved hands, like paws. The first pair hangs from their gnarled shoulders, the second and third pairs nestle up against their misbegotten hips" (Däniken 2010).

The *Gigantomachy* is the story of the battle between the giants, led by Alcyoneus, and the Olympian gods, led by Zeus, and it is perhaps the most widely depicted struggle in Greek art and literary tradition. In this battle, the giants bombard the gods with boulders and the flaming trunks of burning trees. According to the oracle, the gods would be unable to destroy the giants unless a powerful mortal aided them. Of course, in ancient Greece this could be only one individual, the legendary Heracles (Sacks 1995, 92).

Subsequent Greek gods were also giants. Unlike the Gigantes, however, these gods were blond-haired, fair-skinned, and Nordic in appearance. This is consistent with the fact that Caucasians (some of whom were depicted as giants in contemporaneous reports) were once dominant and prevalent in areas long thought to be the sole domain of non-European peoples (Sacks 1995, 92).

Greco-Roman literature is full of stories of giants, which we will explore in greater detail in the next chapter. We will visit the intriguing accounts of the renowned fifth century BCE Greek historian Herodotus as well as the commentaries of other classical writers. Let's turn now to Western Europe to see what their literature, with regard to the existence of giants, may yield.

THE NORSE DEITIES AND THE GIANTS

The Germanic peoples have a rich mythological tradition filled with supernatural creatures, gods, trolls, elves, half gods, and, of course, giants. As such, many parallels can be drawn between Teutonic myths and legends and those of other cultures. Take, for example, the striking similarities between the Norse god Odin and Olle, the tribal god of North America's Tuleyone Indians. Like Odin, Olle is a colossal giant with a horned helmet who is both a god of war and a savior. Olle rescues his people from a fiery demon named Sahte (Joseph 2005).

These Teutonic myths and legends tell us of the earliest beliefs and cosmologies of the ancient Norse and other Germanic peoples of northwestern Europe. In them are visions of the frost giants and *Jötnar*. According to the Eddas, an ancient collection of Norse stories, there are two races of giants: the children of Thrud, who descend from the frost giant Ymir, and the children of Bor, who include the Aesir. Although tremendous in size, the Aesir are distinctly Nordic in appearance. Later, in chapter 4, we will explore some of these Nordic stories in greater detail.

MADAME BLAVATSKY'S LEMURIAN GIANTS

As Scott Corrales rightfully put it in his 2010 essay "The Persistence of Giants," "Any discussion of the role of giant-lore in cryptoarchaeology would be incomplete without mentioning, at least in passing, the Lemurian giants conjured up by Helena Petrovna Blavatsky, the guiding light of the Theosophical movement at the turn of the last century." The Theosophical Movement was Blavatsky's own concoction of Far Eastern mysticism and esoteric knowledge. It combined Judeo-Christian tradition with crude social Darwinism.

According to Blavatsky, "the giant Lemurians stood some 10 to 15 feet tall, had skins resembling alligator hide, faces with protuberant mandibles, small eyes on the sides of their skulls and elongated, double-jointed limbs." Scott Corrales explains:

By her description, Mu was a far cry from the halcyon Atlantis: it was a barren land covered in the emanations of active volcanoes, which caused its colossal inhabitants to live in crude huts made of hardened lava. But Madame Blavatsky improved her creations' lot considerably by adding that with the passing of eons, these towering monsters evolved into the ancestors of the Australian aborigines and other Melanesian peoples.

Blavatsky has become one of the most controversial figures of the last century, and has even been viewed as a forerunner of the Nazi movement, due to her introduction of the Aryan myth as the superior fifth root race of humankind. (It might be noted that the Aryan is also depicted as being a race of light-skinned giants from the lost continent of Atlantis.)

CHINESE MYTHOLOGY: THE STORY OF THE GIANT P'AN KU

As in the Nordic and Celtic myths, a giant was the first living being in Chinese mythology. According to their traditions, in the beginning the entire cosmos was encapsulated by a single egg. Within this egg was a state of utter chaos. The boundaries that distinguish heaven and Earth did not yet exist, and utter darkness reigned, without a sun or moon or stars. From this internal chaotic matter, the first being, the giant P'an Ku emerged. Finding himself trapped in perpetual darkness and chaos, P'an Ku decided to bring order to chaos and create the known universe. His first act as creator of this new cosmos was to break through the egg that surrounded him. "The lighter part of the egg (yang) rose and became the heavens, while the heavier part (yin) fell and became the earth" (Rosenberg 1994, 360).

P'an Ku stood upon the Earth for eighteen thousand years, preventing the sky from crashing to earth by bracing it with his forehead. Eventually P'an Ku lay down and fell asleep, during which time he died. According to mythologist Donna Rosenberg (1994): P'an Ku's head and his eyebrows formed the planets and stars. His left eye formed the sun and his right eye the moon. His flesh formed the soil of the Earth and his blood the oceans and rivers. His teeth and his bones formed rocks, minerals, and gems. His breath formed the clouds and the wind, while his voice became lightning and thunder. His perspiration formed rain and the dew. The hair on his body formed trees, plants, and flowers, while parasites living on his skin became animals and fish.

The similarities between the events of P'an Ku's mythology and the death and dismemberment of Ymir of Nordic literature, and the subsequent creation of the world from his body, are quite apparent. Indeed, even the account of the parasites on P'an Ku's skin becoming animals and fish harkens back to German legend wherein the maggots inside of Ymir's stomach transformed into a race of dwarves.

CHINESE MUMMIES AND THE WATCHERS

In their book *Uriel's Machine,* Christopher Knight and Robert Lomas discuss the so-called *Watchers,* a race of fallen angels who mated with mortal women and produced the giants who came to rule the antediluvian world. Some researchers theorize that these entities were also the progenitors of both the Celtic and Germanic peoples of Western Europe.

The Watchers are featured in the Book of Enoch, where they and their offspring implore Enoch to represent them: "All the giants [and monsters] grew afraid and called Mahway. He came to them and the giants pleaded with him and sent him to Enoch [to speak on their behalf]" (Knight and Lomas 2001, 84). They then beg the god of Newgrange to spare them and the world from the comet about to strike and bring about the mighty deluge. The god responds: "All the mystery had not yet been revealed to you. . . . You have no peace. . . . Behold, destruction is coming, a great flood, and it will destroy all" (Knight and Lomas 2001, 294). Knight and Lomas believe that this culture of Watchers—the giants of biblical fame—knew of the coming catastrophe and felt that they would find safety and salvation only in the Tarim Basin, a high plateau guarded by the mountain ranges of Tibet and Mongolia.

Interestingly enough, a series of Chinese archaeological excavations in the late 1980s revealed hundreds of very tall mummies along the western border of China, the human remains of which exhibited clear Caucasian traits. These are known as the Tarim mummies. One of the taller ones, called Chärchän Man or the Ur-David, was about 6.5 feet in height—and some were even taller. Knight and Lomas assert that, to the Asians who first recorded their encounters with these yellow-haired barbarians, they truly must have seemed like giants, and in this they may have contributed to or given rise to some of the rumors of giants and strange yellow-haired peoples. They do not, however, explain the ancient accounts of monstrous and imposing beings that possessed near-supernatural or even extraterrestrial strength and abilities.

Other ancient corpses discovered in Mongolia, Siberia, and Central Asia display the same European characteristics. While a fair number of these mummies date back to at least 3500 BCE, others are even older, dating to around 5000–4000 BCE. In addition to having European features, they wore Western-style clothing, including plaid twill and the world's earliest known pair of pants. Carbon-14 dating provides perhaps the best estimate of the mummies' age, placing them at 3,500 years before the birth of the Han Chinese civilization in 206 BCE. Evidence suggests that they are related to an Indo-European–speaking group of Caucasians known as the Tocharians (Baumer 2000, 28). These prehistoric Chinese remains were unknown to much of the outside world until a security breach led to the announcement of the discoveries in 1994.

Were these mummies found in Tarim the remains of the Watchers of biblical renown? It's an intriguing question that may never be fully answered. We will elaborate on the mysterious Watchers in chapter 8 because there is much more to be said about these cryptic figures about whom so little is known but about whom much speculation exists.

GIANTS IN THE NEW WORLD: FROM MYTH TO HISTORY

In the earliest written accounts of almost every culture we find descriptions of fierce light-skinned people who were once the central force of a lost civilization. Science writer Terrence Aym, in an e-mail message to the author on January 22, 2011, describes the following series of events in addressing the presence of giants in ancient North America. He also discusses some of the encounters between European explorers and various gigantic Caucasian aborigines in Central and South America.

According to Aym, the Paiute tribe of present-day Nevada tells of an ancient war they waged against a primordial race of white-skinned, red-haired giants. The Paiute claim they were as tall as twelve feet in height and called the imposing Caucasians the *Si-Te-Cah*. (*Si-Te-Cah* literally means "tule-eaters" in the language of the Paiute Indians. *Tule* is a fibrous plant that the giants used to construct assault rafts.) According to tribal lore, this very tall race was already living in North America when the ancestors of the Paiute arrived fifteen thousand years ago. The modern scientific dogmatism dismisses such reports as sheer fantasy, but there has to be more to it than just a case of overactive imagination. And indeed, in the United States, hundreds of excavations, including sites in Virginia, New York state, Michigan, Illinois, Tennessee, Arizona, and Nevada, support the Paiute account.

Hard scientific evidence specifically buttressing the legend of a war with giant red-haired Caucasians first came to light in 1924 at Lovelock Cave in Nevada. According to the legend, during the pitch of battle, the Paiute pursued the giants into a cave, where they took sanctuary and continued to resist the tribe, ignoring their demands to exit the cave and face the tribe head-on. The enraged tribesmen covered the cave with brush and then ignited it into flames, hoping to burn their enemies out. A small number of the stalwart giants ran from the cave entrance and were immediately pummeled by a barrage of arrows. Those who remained in the cave were overcome by intense fumes and perished.

In 1911, skeletons and fossils were found in the area dating to the time of the legend's origin. More than ten thousand artifacts were unearthed, including the mummified remains of two red-haired giants. One of them was a female, 6.5 feet tall, and the other a male that towered over 8 feet. These relics proved once and for all that the Paiute myth of a war against a race of white-skinned, red-haired giants was not fantasy, but was in fact a stark reality. Evidence in the form of broken arrows that had been shot into the cave and a dark layer of burned material confirms the description of the climactic battle scene that concludes the legend.

Two very large skeletons were then unearthed in the Humboldt dry lakebed near Lovelock, Nevada. Among the human remains was one skeleton wrapped in a gum-covered cloth not unlike those found in Egyptian mummifications, and measuring some 8.5 feet tall. The other was an astounding 10 feet tall.

The Book of Mormon, which also speaks of giants, calls these original inhabitants the *Jaredites,* often considered the Olmec of Central America (but it is more than likely that the Olmec were just a single part of a much more widely distributed population). In Ether 15:26, the Mormon scriptures claim that they were "large and mighty men as to the strength of men." The sixteenth-century chronicler Fernando de Alva Cortés Ixtlilxóchitl wrote:

> In this land called New Spain there were giants, as demonstrated by their bones that have been discovered in many areas. The ancient Toltec record keepers referred to the giants as Quinametzin; and as they had a record of the history of the Quinametzinm they learned that they had many wars and dissensions among themselves in this

land that is now called New Spain. They were destroyed, and their civilization came to an end as a result of great calamities and as a punishment from the heavens for graves [sic] sins that they had committed. (Allen and Allen 2008, 124)

From the evidence, it seems irrefutable that a real race of red-haired giants dominated the Americas at one time, perhaps tens of thousands of years before the arrival of the ancestors of today's Native Americans across the Bering Strait some thirteen thousand to fifteen thousand years ago. In defense of this statement, one must concede that race is a mutable thing, and that the physical appearance of New World humans during the Ice Age may have been quite different—perhaps they were part of a line that left no known descendants. By the same token, the presence of a forgotten Caucasian population in Asia that could have walked across Beringia with the other Asiatics is also a possibility. This would explain some of the unusual results from recent genetic testing, which has confirmed the presence of Caucasoid genes in some of the existing ancient remains.

Western European explorers such as Ferdinand Magellan, Sir Francis Drake, Hernando de Soto, and Commodore Byron (the famous poet Lord Byron's grandfather) all reported encountering living giants all across the North American continent, remnants of a once proud and noble race of Caucasian "superhumans."

Later, in chapter 6, we will explore more accounts of giants in the New World, but first let's examine what may have been one of their early roles in the history of the human race. We will then attempt to define a viable scientific explanation for the genesis of giants. Where did the giants come from? If not the stars, did they evolve on Earth and, if so, how? We will examine both topics in the following chapter.

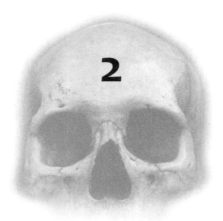

An Early Role of Giants and a Catalyst for Their Genesis

GIANTS: BUILDERS OF ANCIENT CIVILIZATIONS?

In the earliest accounts, which are most prevelant in the Greek and Near Eastern tradition, giants of prehistory are often depicted as great builders and engineers. Of all the structures left to us by the ancients, perhaps the most enduring are those that are universally known as megalithic monuments. These great architectural achievements are compelling, not only because of their immense size, but also because of the ambiguity concerning their origins.

Who built them, when, why, and, equally important, how? In European folklore, giants were often credited with creating these massive stone monoliths. Indeed, there is direct mythological connection between giants, the prehistoric construction of these megalithic structures, and the eventual doom of a lost civilization. In this chapter we will explore the open-ended question of the early role that giants may have played, before moving on to examine a potential scientific cause for gigantism. We may come up with some very surprising answers.

ACCOUNTS OF GIANTS AS SKILLED ENGINEERS

In the Book of Numbers, Moses sent a preinvasion reconnaissance into the Promised Land to gather intelligence about the Canaanite enemy. The scouts reached as far as Hebron, where they found, much to their surprise and horror, that the "descendants of Anak"* were still inhabiting the region. Pioneering biblical archaeologist G. Ernest Wright addresses this issue of giants in ancient Canaan in his 1938 article "Troglodytes and Giants in Palestine." In it he writes:

> Pausanias [a second-century CE Greek geographer] tells us that the great walls of Mycenae, Tiryns and Argos were constructed by the giant Cyclopes. . . . Hebrews viewing some of the cities of Canaan, which we now know to have possessed walls as thick as eighteen feet, and often built of cyclopean masonry, might well have thought in terms of giants, just as did the Greeks.

Biblical expert Ronald S. Hendel corroborates this view in the March/April 2009 edition of *Biblical Archaeology Review,* in which he writes that when the Israelites were confronted with the vast "cyclopean" walls of the "old, ruined Canaanite cities" they inevitably concluded that the indigenous population of Canaan did in fact consist primarily of giants. "This conclusion," says Hendel "is borne out by many Biblical texts." When the spies returned to their equally horrified

---

*This reference to the Anak relates directly to the Anakin, which is a variant of Anunnaki. Allegedly the Anunnaki were giants who created humans as slave labor through a targeted mutation in the DNA of *Homo erectus.* Zecharia Sitchin identified the Anunnaki with extraterrestrials from the planet Nibiru. (We will have more on the work of Zecharia Sitchin later.)

commander and prophet, Moses, they reported: "The people who live in the land are powerful, and their fortified cities are very large, and indeed we saw giants there. . . . All the people that we saw in it are men of great height. . . . We seemed in our own eyes like grasshoppers, and so we seemed in their eyes" (Hendel 2009).

For the most part it is naturally easier to place ancient reports in a modern context and assume that the original writers simply were confused or didn't know what they were talking about. That seems unlikely, however, because these cultures were highly sophisticated. Although they were not as advanced as the culture of Atlantis, they were probably more or less on a par with our own culture today. When they made conscientious descriptions of people, places, and events, they were not doing so as children—they were making intelligent and highly rational interpretations of what they were witnessing. So yes, it is highly likely that the people of Canaan were indeed "giants," as described by these spies in the Old Testament.

Hendel also mentions the Battle of Jericho—a racial cleansing of the Canaanites at the hands of the Israelites wherein the city of Jericho was destroyed and hundreds of thousands of Canaanite men, women, and children were killed. As stated in Joshua 6:20: "Joshua and his troops marched around the city once a day for six days; on the seventh day they marched around it seven times, and on the seventh circuit they blew their horns and shouted. When the people heard the sound of the horns, the people shouted a mighty shout, and the walls fell down." It was creations such as the walls of Jericho that best illustrate the building capability of the early giants; however, from this quotation we see that even masonry allegedly built by them wasn't totally indefensible.

The ancient historian Josephus confirms that these "giants"* were indeed skilled architects. He mentions two pillars, one of stone and one

---

*British author Harold T. Wilkins later identified these giants as the "giants of the kingdom of Thoth, or Taut of Atlantis" (Wilkins 1952, 404–5).

of very hard brick, which the giants erected to stand as a lasting testament to their engineering skills. Two were constructed so that at least one might survive the great deluge to come. The giants feared that this final catastrophe would destroy everything that had been built by their hands (Childress 2010).

In *The Antiquities of the Jews,* Book 1, Josephus wrote:

> Now, these pillars remain in the land of Siriad to this day. . . . Noah quitted the land of Seth for fear that his family might be annihilated by the giants. . . . As late as the days of Joshua, son of Nun, there were still giants of Hebron, who had bodies so large and faces so entirely different from other men, that they were surprising to the sight and terrible to the hearing. The bones of these giant men are still shown to this day. (Childress 2010)

DID GIANTS BUILD THE DOLMENS OF WESTERN EUROPE?

The medieval Danish historian Saxo Grammaticus insisted that giants must have once existed, because only they, with their awesome strength and superhuman capabilities, could have built the dolmens, menhirs, massive walls, and other structures that are strewn across Western Europe.

The idea of a vast megalithic culture that once dominated much of Europe in the remote past is taken up by the author Paul Dunbavin in his book *Atlantis of the West.* For Dunbavin, the megalithic structures of Europe are not just simple creations built by a Stone Age culture, but the sophisticated handiwork of an advanced and ancient race, possibly the Atlanteans. (Indeed, Britain was once named Albion, after a Titan king of Atlantis.) Dunbavin believes that Atlantis lies beneath the Irish Sea and was submerged in 3100 BCE when a comet struck Earth, causing the Earth's crust to shift and thus shrinking some of the existing landmasses, including those in and around ancient Europe (Dunbavin 2003).

ARMENIAN STONEHENGE

Located on a rocky promontory near Sissian in Armenia is the profoundly ancient site of Zorats Karer, also known as Karahunj, which has been dubbed the Armenian Stonehenge. It dates to approximately 7600–4500 BCE, and as such, is probably the oldest stone circle in Europe. The rocks of this circle are quite large and extremely heavy. Extensive research carried out by Paris Herouni and Elma Parsamyan of the Biurakan Observatory has led them to conclude that the site was dedicated to the Armenian sun god Ari in that some of the stones mirror the brightest star of the Cygnus constellation—Deneb. Tellingly, some old Armenian folktales tell of a distant epoch when the sun god Ari ordered a fallen race of giants to move the immense blocks of stone to the site and construct it.

The question of whether Zorats Karer could be the oldest observatory of its kind in Europe, if not the world, was taken up by Oxford astrophysicist Mihran Vardanyan. He agrees that this site was no doubt an ancient observatory, but also suggests that it may well have been an ancient necropolis:

> The most commonly accepted theory about the meaning of Karahunj is that it is an ancient burial ground, or necropolis—a place to act as a bridge between the earth and the heavens in the cyclical journey of the soul involving life, death and rebirth. The necropolis thesis is certainly true for after our initial investigations of the central circle, it is clear the site was aligned to the sun, most likely aligned to the moon and—what is really exciting, possibly even some stars or planets—owing to the placement of small holes drilled through the monoliths and aimed at the horizon. It is these holes

which makes this exceptional megalithic site unique out of all similar European sites. (Vardanyan 2011)

In December 2010, the popular History channel documentary series *Ancient Aliens* featured Zorats Karer on episode 14, "Unexplained Structures." The show linked Herouni and Parsamyan's Deneb theory with the discovery of three hundred exoplanets by NASA's Kepler planet-finding satellite within the Cygnus constellation (History 2010). This connection, without a doubt, is truly sensational and demands further investigation.

THE FALLEN TEMPLE OF BAALBEK

One of the most ancient and archaeologically significant megalithic sites in the world is Baalbek,* where the bones of what may be ancient giants have been found. Baalbek lies approximately eighty-six kilometers northeast of the city of Beirut in eastern Lebanon. This most enigmatic of holy places is one of the Near East's most important Roman and pre-Roman temple sites of study by historians and archaeologists. In 1898, a German expedition there claimed to have discovered no evidence of occupation prior to the Roman period, despite other claims suggesting a very ancient habitation of the site.

Recent archaeological finds have supported the latter idea, for in a deep trench at the edge of the Jupiter temple platform, Neolithic artifacts were discovered, along with the skeletons of three individuals of giant stature! Pottery dating to the Seleucid era (323–64 BCE) as well as Roman era remains (64 BCE–312 CE) were also discovered.

---

*The origin of the name Baalbek remains a mystery. It may derive from the Phoenician term *Baal,* which simply means "lord" or "god." The name was later applied to a Semitic sky god that predominated throughout the ancient Near East. According to ancient mythology, Baalbek was actually the birthplace of Baal himself, and it is highly probable that Baal was the central figure in a trinity of gods venerated at the site—including his son, Aliyan, and his daughter, Anat.

During both the Seleucid and Roman occupations, the town surrounding the immense religious monument was known as Heliopolis, the "City of the Sun," and the sun god Jupiter was the focal point of the shrine. (The Roman god Jupiter had overtaken and supplanted the Greek god Zeus, and replaced the earlier god Baal, who incidentally shared some common characteristics with Zeus and, subsequently, Jupiter.)

Archaeologists now agree that Baalbek is more than nine thousand years old, with continual settlement dating from the Neolithic Age to the Roman Iron Age. Surrounding the site are massive walls built with twenty-four monoliths, weighing some three hundred tons each. The tallest wall, on the western flank of the temple site, contains what is known as the *trilithon*, a row of three stones, each 19 meters long, 4.3 meters high, and 3.6 meters broad, cut from solid limestone. Each stone weighs approximately eight hundred tons. Even with today's technology, moving them into place would be a tremendous architectural accomplishment indeed.

According to David Hatcher Childress (2000): "Large numbers of pilgrims came from Mesopotamia as well as the Nile Valley to the Temple of Ba'al-Astarte. The site is mentioned in the Bible in the *Book of Kings*. There is a vast underground network of passages beneath the acropolis. Their function is unknown, but they were possibly used to shelter pilgrims, probably at a later period."

How then was Baalbek constructed? Ancient Arab writings explain that the first stages of Baalbek, including the trilithon and other massive stone blocks, were built following the Great Flood at the mandate of King Nimrod, by a "tribe of giants" (Childress 2000). Again, we see the same giant motif, lending credence to the race of giants theory. How could so many disparate cultures in so many isolated locations all around the world arrive at the same supposition: giants were responsible for building the great megalithic monuments of prehistory.

STONEHENGE: THE GIANTS' RING?

Another significant megalithic site needs little introduction. We are referring, of course, to the glorious Stonehenge, perhaps the most famous megalithic structure in the world.

One fascinating story concerning Stonehenge is a twelfth-century account written by Geoffrey of Monmouth in his work *Historia Regum Britanniae,* also known as *The History of the Kings of Britain.* Geoffrey maintained that the rocks of Stonehenge were healing rocks that had been imported from Africa and that they had immense curative properties. Collectively called the Giant's dance, Stonehenge had, according to Geoffrey, originally been constructed on Mount Killaraus in Ireland.

The fifth-century Arthur-like figure Ambrosius Aurelius, at the behest of Merlin, designated Stonehenge to be instead a monument for the knights who perished fighting off Saxon incursions. Thus, the king dispatched Merlin, Uther Pendragon, and fifteen thousand knights to Ireland to capture the monument and bring it back to Britain. The knights slew seven thousand Irish warriors, but were unable to move the rocks with ropes and brute force. Then something very strange happened. Using the power of sound, Merlin dismantled the stones and transported them through a dimensional rift directly to Salisbury, where they were reassembled using levitation. Ambrosius Aurelius then died and was buried within Stonehenge, which is also known as the "Giants' Ring of Stonehenge."

Until recently there has been no accurate method for pinpointing when the stones were quarried and erected. However, a new dating method known as chlorine-23 has now been developed. Recent attempts at using this new method on Stonehenge have revealed that the monument, far from being only 4,500 years old as is maintained by current academia, in actual fact dates to 25,000 BCE.

Mainstream scientists have rejected these figures and, subsequently, do not consider this method of dating to be reliable. However, the method is deemed to be highly accurate. (Except when it contradicts what the establishment wants to believe as opposed to what the facts clearly point to!) In rebuttal, established academicians claim that the proponents of chlorine-23 themselves are merely seeing what they want to believe, in a total reversal of the truth!

DID GIANTS CONSTRUCT CARNAC?

The Basques of southern France and northern Spain are descended from an ancient people. According to genetic profiling begun in the late twentieth century, their bloodlines go back some forty thousand years, to the continent's first modern population of *Homo sapiens:* Cro-Magnons. Part of the evidence for this is their existence as a truly unique population, with no known linguistic, cultural, or genetic relatives anywhere in Europe.

The Basques have a unique mythology as well. According to Basque accounts, giants are responsible for constructing one of the most enigmatic series of stone monuments in Western Europe: Carnac in Brittany, France. About Carnac, author and scholar David Hatcher Childress has this to say (2010): "Carnac holds the greatest concentration of megaliths in the world. Conservative estimates claim that megaliths were being erected here by 5000 BCE, [over] seven thousand years ago. They may be much older."

Childress elaborates: "Much of the gigantic astronomical observatory is probably under water. Many of the megaliths along the Brittany coast are apparently submerged. Many famous sites actually lead into the water, and some megaliths can be seen at low tide when they are barely above the surface." Given this, it could very well be that these sunken ruins were above water prior to a deluge, perhaps that of the Great Flood. Indeed, as Childress adds: "Many of the long lines of standing stones at Carnac and around the Morbihan Gulf were apparently built when the geography of Brittany was quite different" (Childress 2010).

Francis Hitching, another noted scholar on the subject and the author of a seminal book about it—*Earth Magic*—believes that the complex must have contained a central sighting megalith from which to observe moonrises and moonsets. Indeed, the whole series of structures seems to be a vast astronomical observatory in that it is viewable from space, seeming to proclaim "Here we are!" to any life that may be far above us in the skies.

IF SO . . . HOW?

Based on the examples of megalithic construction listed in this chapter, it is clear that our ancestors may have had contact with another, more "advanced" earthborn culture. This more advanced culture was, by many mythological accounts, composed of giants, who in my opinion, either constructed the prehistoric megalithic structures or influenced their building by handing down superior technology by which to construct them.

All of this begs the tantalizing question: Did giants really exist? And if so, how would it be scientifically possible that they did? We will now turn our attention to this most pressing of questions in order to shed light on the enigmatic origins of ancient giants.

THE WELTEISLEHRE AND ITS COSMIC RAYS

The cosmic ice theory, also known as the world ice theory, or Welteislehre, was presented to the skeptical intelligentsia of Europe in 1929 in a book called *Glazial-Kosmogonie,* written by mining engineer Hans Hoerbiger and a schoolteacher named Philip Fauth. This cosmic ice theory states that world history—indeed the entire existence of the Earth itself—includes a legacy of cataclysmic events initiated by the interaction of ice and other natural elements (The Gnostic Liberation Front 2003).

The solar system began, in the Hoerbigerians' view, with the collision of two stellar objects, a supergiant star and a smaller body, perhaps a dead sun or a gigantic comet, that was soaking wet to the core with water. When the smaller star, or comet, crashed into the supergiant, the heat of the latter vaporized the water and other elements as huge chunks of the star spewed into space. These chunks eventually formed a system of rings that became the Milky Way. Out of this ring system, our solar system, one of many, was born (Gnostic Liberation Front 2003).

During this primeval stage, our solar system had many more planets than exist at present, and the gas giants and their planet-sized moons existed in different locations. It is plausible that at one time there were multiple suns within the solar system (Gnostic Liberation Front 2003). It is also plausible that many of the worlds in the solar system, now barren and lifeless, once were home not only to life, but to other civilizations as well.

The evolutionary history of our solar system is long and complex. For countless eons the orbits of the outer planets were in decay, and one by one they plummeted toward the planets in the inner solar system, including the Earth. This is due to a significant amount of hydrogen between the planetary orbits. From beyond the orbit of Neptune, huge interplanetary icebergs in a trajectory toward Earth and the sun have caused many of Earth's natural disasters. The arrival of these interplanetary icebergs is heralded by hailstorms and sunspots, and if and when they smash into the sun, they produce a blanket of vapor and thin ice that covers the inner planets, wreaking havoc on them (Gnostic Liberation Front 2003). These disasters are the basis of many of the flood myths and end-times legends so prevalent in the Hindu, Teutonic, Christian, and pre-Columbian American traditions.

The Earth has had many natural satellites (or moons) since its formation eighteen billion years ago. These moons were once planets but were captured by the Earth's gravity, and they spiraled into Earth's gravitational field until they disintegrated and were swallowed up by the Earth, becoming part of the planet's geography. This is evidenced in the geologic record. The rock strata, when examined, show the full history of this cosmic evolutionary process.

The most recent episode of moon-Earth collision occurred when the Cenozoic moon fell from the sky, and the present moon, Luna, took its place. This event resides in the collective racial memory of the human species and manifests in the great myths and legends related to mass destruction, galactic battles, and the end of the world, most notably in Ragnarok and the Book of Revelation (Chouinard 2008, 450).

Hans Schindler Bellamy, a loyal follower of Hoerbiger and a British citizen during the mid-twentieth century, created the basis of pre-Luna culture, a term comparable to "antediluvian" or "pre-Flood" culture currently used by Christian creationists. During the age of the fall of the Cenozoic moon, the moon pulled the oceans into a "girdle tide" as it fell into the Earth's surface. This, according to Bellamy and Hoerbiger, forced many advanced civilizations to seek refuge in mountaintops and highlands such as Tibet and the Andes (Gnostic Liberation Front 2003).

Meanwhile, much of the Earth was thrust into an ice age. The new moon, Luna, now loomed close in the sky, and its rapid revolutions around the Earth, nearly six times a day, resulted in eclipses of the sun. Bellamy believes that this is where so many of our Norse and Christian legends about the end of the world come from, and why the idea of demons and powers of mass destruction permeate so much of humanity's cultural lore.

As the old moon disintegrated, the new moon, Luna, finally settled into a regular orbit around Earth. Then there was a long period of tranquility and virtual paradise, followed by more horrendous events that may have led to the destruction of Atlantis (Gnostic Liberation Front 2003).

The period in which Luna's gravity pulled heaviest on the primordial Earth is the time when the greatest number of gigantic creatures are found in the fossil record, including evidence of giant-sized humanoid footprints. The formation of these giants may have been due to radiation from the stronger cosmic rays that were part and parcel of this changing moonscape.

In Peter Kolosimo's book *Timeless Earth,* he notes these Earth changes:

> The tides will become stronger, thus flooding great continental areas, and, as a second consequence, human beings and creatures in general will become taller. According to these two scientists [Denis Saurat and H. S. Bellamy, the two chief disciples of Hoerbiger] this is the only possible explanation of the huge species of plants and animals that have existed on earth, and of a race of men sixteen feet tall. The increase of men's stature, and likewise of their intelligence, is also due, according to this theory, to an increase in the intensity of cosmic rays. (1973, 27)

COSMIC RAYS: THE DRIVING FORCE BEHIND GIANT MUTATION?

Kolosimo also writes:

> There has been, and will continue to be, much animated discussion of the nature and effect of these rays. Years and years of experiment will be necessary before firm conclusions can be reached. Professor Jakob Eugster, the greatest expert on the subject, has remarked that "Like other radiations, such as wireless telegraphy, X-rays, etc, cosmic rays may have two types of effect: they may cause mutations, i.e.,

changes in inherited characteristics, and also damage or alteration in tissues." (1973, 27)

To conclude his argument, Kolosimo states: "It is true that the earth has had moons that have been destroyed, and if the result has been to increase the intensity with which the human beings are bombarded by radioactive particles, this may be certainly a contributory cause of the phenomenon of gigantism" (1973, 27–28).

Kolosimo then cited the Mont Pelee explosion of 1902 on the West Indian island of Martinique, which in the city of Saint Pierre alone caused some twenty thousand deaths. A dense cloud of purple gases and aqueous vapors were emitted by the volcanic crater and were seen drifting over its summit and toward populated regions of the island. Then a pillar of fire blasted forth from the volcano to a height of 1,300 feet, setting the gaseous cloud ablaze. The mass of fire and vapor burning at 1,000 degrees centigrade obliterated the entire population of the island, except one convict protected by the safety of his prison walls (Kolosimo 1973, 28).

The city of Saint Pierre was razed to the ground. Nothing remained of its former glory, and the city itself was never rebuilt. However, life did return to the ashen ruins sooner than was expected. But it was life on an immense scale. Plants and animals grew to an exceptional size. Mammals, reptiles, amphibians, even spiders and insects were of considerably larger size—giants in comparison to their smaller predecessors. These mutations were attributed to intense, cosmic-ray-like radiation that gathered deep within the volcano. During the immense volcanic explosion, radioactive material rained down upon the unsuspecting island inhabitants.

Indeed, humans too, were affected. Kolosimo states that the "director of the research center, Dr. Jules Graveure, became two and a half inches taller, and his assistant, Dr. Rouen, aged 59, grew by about two inches" (Kolosimo 1973, 28). The radiation released by this volcanic eruption had been hidden deep within the planet since the beginning of the planet itself.

Numerous scientists have studied the source of this awesome radioactivity, but one in particular has made a substantial attempt to describe its terrestrial origins. In *Cosmos* by Carl Sagan, the issue of cosmic rays and solar radiation was promptly addressed. According to Sagan, these forces are the wellspring of all life on this planet:

> The origin and evolution of life are connected in the most intimate way with the origin and evolution of the stars. First: The very matter of which we are composed, the atoms that make life possible, were generated long ago and far away in giant red stars. The relative abundance of the chemical elements found in the Cosmos matches the relative abundance of atoms generated in stars so well as to leave little doubt that red giants and supernovae are the ovens and crucibles in which matter has been forged. The Sun is a second- or third-generation star. All the matter in it, all the matter you see around you, has been through one or two previous cycles of stellar alchemy. Second: The existence of certain varieties of heavy atoms on the Earth suggest there was a nearby supernova explosion shortly before the solar system was formed. But this is unlikely; more likely, the shock wave produced by the supernova compressed interstellar gas and dust and triggered the condensation of the solar system. Third: When the Sun turned on, its ultraviolet radiation poured into the atmosphere of the Earth; its warmth generated lightning; and these energy sources sparked the complex organic molecules that led to the origin of life. Fourth: Life on Earth runs almost exclusively on sunlight. Plants gather the photons and convert solar to chemical energy. Animals parasitize the plants. Farming is simply the methodical harvesting of sunlight, using plants as grudging intermediaries. We are, almost all of us, solar-powered. Finally, the hereditary changes called mutations provide the raw material for evolution. Mutations, from which nature selects its new inventory of life-forms, are produced in part by cosmic rays—high-energy particles ejected at almost the speed of light in

supernova explosions. The evolution of life on Earth is driven in part by the spectacular deaths of distant, massive suns. (1980)

Some mainstream scientists readily accept the cosmic ray theory with regard to gigantism because it is known that gigantism in both plant and animal species spearheads evolutionary changes. Radiation causing mutations of gigantic proportions also was widely rampant in the movies of mid-twentieth-century Hollywood—films haunted by the real possibility of an atomic catastrophe. But these calamities are far from fictional, far from merely a theory—they really happened.

Kolosimo writes: "During the first phase of its existence the sun must have poured forth a stupendous volume of radiation on all its satellite planets: even today, the intensity of radiation goes hand in hand with the occurrence of sun-storms."(1973, 29) Kolosimo further speculates that "gigantism must have been a feature of life on earth from very early times, and not only in the Triassic period," which began some 180 million years ago.

This was an age of great prehistoric reptiles and the dawn of the first dinosaurs, which succeeded the more primitive mammal-like reptiles and supercrocodile species. But in an attempt to fairly evaluate the full extent of the influence of cosmic rays on plant and animal gigantism, Kolosimo admits:

Cosmic rays, it is true, are filtered through the earth's atmosphere, which must have been much denser in early times. But it can hardly have been so dense as to affect radiation greatly, since at the present day rays of this type traverse the human body in incredible quantities—some 650,000 to the minute; they can penetrate massive walls of lead, or sea water to a depth of 3,500 feet. The conclusion is, then, that cosmic rays would not in themselves have sufficed to create a race of giants, though they may certainly have helped to do so. (1973, 29)

It seems highly likely that cosmic rays may have been a contributing cause to the phenomenon of gigantism in ancient days. Although this may never be fully proved, there is a lot to learn in the exploration of the question. Perhaps we may glean more as we continue our conversation about the remains of giants in the fossil record the world over. Toward that end, in the next chapter we will examine tales and findings of giants in the Mediterranean region and Asia Minor. We have a lot of fascinating ground to cover, and no doubt we will unearth some very interesting anomalies.

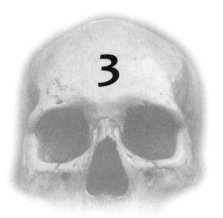

3

Accounts of Giants in the Classical Sources

As we shall learn, according to Greek myth as conceived by such seminal authors as Hesiod and Homer, the primordial Earth produced a series of primeval monsters and giant humanlike beings known as Titans, who became the first race of Greek gods. Other giants followed, including the Cyclopes, Gigantes, Centaurs, and Typhons. In this chapter we will examine ancient evidence of them, primarily from sources derived from the classical world, and explore how the inhabitants of the classical world were on a very physical search to find evidence for themselves that these giants once roamed the Earth.

A LAND OF GODS AND MONSTERS

The ancient Greek writers called their country "a land of gods and monsters," referring to the often pernicious Greek deities and the hundreds of various giants, monsters, demigods, and other creatures that inhabited it. These giants, however, such as the Cyclopes, Antaeus, and Orion, were surprisingly humanlike, and they were not "altogether disproportioned to human beings, for they mingled in love and strife with them" (Bulfinch 2004, 115). But those other giants who waged war against the gods and exhibited superhuman, even near godlike, powers were far more gigantic in size than their weaker brethren.

Examples of these gigantic giants include Tityus, who was said to have been so large that while resting on the plain near Mount Olympus, his massive body covered some nine acres. Enceladus, too, required the whole of Mount Aetna upon which to rest his enormous head. Still others, like Briareus, had one hundred arms. Typhon, the sea beast, excreted fire from his abominable lungs.

Bulfinch explains that according to the Romans:

> At one time they put the gods to such fear that they fled into Egypt and hid themselves under various forms. Jupiter took the form of a ram, whence he was afterwards worshipped as the god Ammon with curved horns. Venus a fish, Mercury a bird. At another time the giants attempted to climb up into heaven and for that purpose took up the mountain Ossa and piled it on Pelion. They were at last subdued by thunderbolts, which Minerva invented and taught Vulcan and his Cyclops to make for Jupiter. (2004, 115–16)

The Greek religious writer Hesiod describes the giants vividly. They were warriors of immense strength and power who donned gleaming white armor and brandished long spears and other deadly weapons, treated with poison. These depictions of the giants as cruel combatants adept at the art of war conform to later portrayals in ancient Greek and Roman art. The idea of a revolt against the gods, however, did not emerge until the sixth century BCE, with the first artistic depictions of the conflict. While the poet Hesiod often makes clear that the giants were highly warlike and violent creatures, there was no evidence of those tendencies being directed at the Olympians until a much later time.

BACKING UP THE MYTHS WITH SCIENCE: EXCAVATING GIANT BONES IN ANTIQUITY

Having touched on a few mythological accounts of giants, let's now turn for a brief moment to the field of archaeology. Here we will see how the physical evidence may or may not support the mythological accounts, while bearing in mind that the results of any study regarding the examination of ancient remains purported to be those of ancient giants must be met with caution, but also with an open and prepared mind. Too frequently we are duped by archaeological hoaxes, but an equal amount of discoveries are inexplicable and in this, remain fascinating in their open-ended implications. The findings that you will read about next, culled from *The First Fossil Hunters,* written by historian and folklorist Adrienne Mayor, are some brief examples of the latter.

Contrary to popular belief, the field of archaeology didn't emerge in just the past few centuries. In Jerusalem in the late first century CE, shortly after the crushing defeat of the Jewish revolt at the hands of Titus, the Jewish historian Josephus tells us a new practice became popular: Natural historians, the ancient forerunners of our modern scientists, were digging up giant bones that they then examined, documented, and cataloged. These were the rudimentary beginnings of what would eventually become the fields of archaeology and paleontology.

These early fossil specimens were among those identified as belonging to the great heroes of antiquity. Examples include Theseus, Heracles, Achilles, Ajax, and the various gods and monsters described in many Greek and Roman legends. Such noted classical scholars as Plato and Herodotus back up the theory that these bones belonged to giants, for according to their accounts, the bones that the early archaeologists exhumed from the ground did not belong to any normal human or animal.

Skeptics claim that what the ancients really found were the bones of long-extinct mammals and dinosaurs, such as the mammoth or triceratops. Wherever the truth may lie, for mainstream scholars the choice is simple: Either ancient peoples mistook prehistoric remains of dinosaurs or extinct mammals to be those of the giants and heroes described in their ancient myths—such as the Nephilim as described in the Bible, or the Greeks' very own Titans and Cyclopes—or they downright imagined that they were the remains of giants because they wanted to believe this was so.

In any event, the compelling nature of these unearthed bones caused a great "bone rush" among the people of the city-states of ancient Greece and, later, among the larger territories of the Roman Empire. We will have more to say on this bone rush a bit later in the chapter, but for now let's look at more of the classical accounts that mention giants, before we explore how the concept of giants fits within the cosmology of our classical forebears.

HOMER'S GIANTS

The ancient Greeks possessed a mythology rich in symbolism about giants. In 400 BCE, the Greek poet Homer wrote: "On the earth there once were giants." To the ancient Greeks, Homer was much more than one of their most highly revered writers. In their view, his two principle works, the *Iliad* and the *Odyssey,* were divinely inspired. Together they formed the bible of the entire ancient Greek civilization.

With regard to giants in the *Iliad,* a scenario mentioned briefly by Homer in this work involves the twin giants Otus and Ephialtes. Known collectively as the Aloeidae, they were renowned for their strength and bravery; however, they were equally disdained for their audacity and recklessness.

Otus and Ephialtes brought much chaos upon the gods. They tried to storm the home of the gods by piling three Greek mountains on top of one another—Olympus, Ossa, and Pelion. Ares, god of war, attempted to halt their advance, but instead the giants put Ares in chains and held him captive for thirteen months. Hermes eventually rescued Ares, but it was the goddess Artemis who finally brought about the twin giants' destruction. She metamorphosed into a deer and jumped in front of them. They raised their bows and took aim, each firing a shot, but ultimately they missed the deer and hit each other instead, whereupon both were killed.

In the *Odyssey,* we are introduced to the mighty Cyclopes—a fierce race of one-eyed giants—when Odysseus and his fellow Achaeans became trapped in a cave inhabited by one of the Cyclopes named Polyphemus, who immediately began to devour one of the captives. The air became filled with a heavy-laden stench as the giant gulped down their limbs and torsos in outpourings of blood. The horrifying clamor of agonizing shrieks and crunching bones drowned out the sound of ocean surf and seagulls on the beach. In response, Odysseus's men prayed to Zeus for salvation, but to no avail.

The bloodthirsty giant then murdered two more men. When Polyphemus left in the morning, he placed an immense rock behind him, blocking the exit from the cave. This prevented the Achaeans from following him out to the fields and to safety. Unable to escape and return to the ship, Odysseus planned a ruse. When the giant returned, Odysseus offered his captor wine, intoxicating him. In the morning, as the Cyclops slept, the men gouged out his single eye with a pole. The giant immediately awoke, screaming in agony and calling out to the other Cyclopes for help; however, they simply ignored him. Polyphemus removed the rock blocking the entrance to the cave as he searched blindly for his assailants, and then the Achaeans made their escape.

After escaping the island of the mighty Cyclopes, the Achaeans were caught in a tempest and blown off course. They rowed to the land of the

Laestrygonians, a powerful race of giants. Their giant-king Antiphates and his queen captured and dined on Odysseus's men, who beat a hasty retreat back to their boats as the towering giants hurled immense boulders at them. All of them but for Odysseus were destroyed. Then Odysseus escaped to the home of the goddess Circe, where he remained for some time.

Today it is uncertain whether a man named Homer really existed or the name merely represents a number of separate authors, their individual identities now lost to the sands of time. Despite such speculation, one thing is certain: Homer has proven to be much more than the creator of fairy tales. In his greatest epic, the *Iliad,* the Greeks were pitted against the inhabitants of Troy. This was proven to be a very real, very ancient city by Heinrich Schliemann in the nineteenth century, as we shall read about later in this book.

THE GIANT ORION: ANCIENT BRUTE OR TRAVELER TO THE STARS?

In Pliny the Elder's immortal work *Natural History,* he cites Greek and Roman mythology with regard to an ancient legend. The giant Orion, Pliny explains, was born from the skin of an ox, which had been placed by a humble peasant into the soil of Boeotia. At the insistence of the Atlantean gods Neptune, Mercury, and Jupiter, the Atlantean demigods relieved themselves upon the pile, thereby spawning the giant. Orion is featured at the feet of a bull among the constellations, the bull being the most sacred object of worship among the Atlanteans and their ancient temples (Wilkins 1952, 45).

Orion is not a hideous ogre, however. He is described as very handsome, and he is also said to be a superb and mighty hunter. Orion's main love interest was Merope—the daughter of Oenopion, king of Chios—and he desired to marry her. He purged the island of all beasts and wild creatures, and the spoils of the hunt were given to her as presents in an attempt to win her over. Oenopion, however, refused to grant permission for Orion to marry his daughter. Angered by this, Orion attempted to rape Merope.

This infuriated her father. He made Orion drunk, then robbed him of his vision and guided him to the seashore and left him there. The wandering hero, now blind, followed the sound of a Cyclops hammer until he finally arrived at Lemnos and came to the forge of Hephaestus, who, taking pity on him, entrusted him with one his men, a guide named Kedalion, who took him to the abode of the sun. Orion placed Kedalion on his shoulder and proceeded east, where he met the sun god Helios, who restored his vision with a beam of solar rays.

After this, Orion became the lover and fellow hunter of Artemis. He was her favorite, and she often boasted that one day she would marry the handsome giant. Her brother, Apollo, was highly indignant about the affair, but it didn't deter Orion and his beloved Artemis. One day, as Artemis was out hunting with her bow and arrow, Orion submerged into the sea, with just the top of his head sticking out of the water. Apollo and Artemis happened upon the scene. Apollo knew that what they saw in the water was the head of Orion, but Artemis did not. When Apollo suggested to Artemis that she try to hit the object with an arrow, she complied. She was then horrified to find the dead body of Orion washing up on shore.

Artemis placed him among the stars, where we can still see him today, appearing as a giant, with a girdle, sword, lion's skin, and club. He is followed by his dog, Sirius, and before him fly the Pleiades, who were nymph companions of Artemis.

THE SHOULDER BLADE OF PELOPS

This fascinating story involves the Greeks during the siege of Troy, circa 1200 BCE. According to author and classical scholar Adrienne Mayor, the battle between the ancient Greeks and the inhabitants of

Troy continued unabated for more than a decade—ten long years of bloodshed and misery with no end in sight. At this point the battle-weary Greeks took a Trojan seer prisoner and forced him to reveal ancient secrets. According to the old man, the Greeks would never taste victory unless they located the shoulder blade of the great hero Pelops and brought it to Troy as a talisman. The Greeks then dispatched a vessel to Olympia to find and bring back Pelops's gigantic shoulder blade to the battlefront.

Mayor makes reference to Pausanias, a Greek traveler and geographer of the second century CE, who lived in the times of Emperors Hadrian, Antoninus Pius, and Marcus Aurelius. Mayor says that according to Pausanias, some bones of heroic size were discovered by the Greeks who were searching for the shoulder blade of Pelops, and they assumed that they were his.* These cyclopean relics—believed to possess potent magical and supernatural powers—were found housed in a bronze chest and stored within the Temple of Artemis at Olympia.

Mayor points out in *The First Fossil Hunters* that, according to Pausanias, as a youth Pelops had been chopped up and served to the gods as a blood sacrifice, but once the gods realized on whom they dined, they restored the young Pelops to life. His shoulder bone, however, had already been eaten, so they gave the young hero a new shoulder blade made of ivory. It was this new shoulder blade that was housed with the rest of Pelops's bones in the Temple of Artemis (Mayor 2000).

Pausanias claims that the ivory shoulder bone was actually shipped to Troy during the prolonged war, and Mayor corroborates that account. According to her, it was "bundled in straw for its journey by mule from Olympia to Cyllene on the coast. There it was loaded onto a boat bound

---

*Mythologically speaking, Pelops was the great-grandfather of the Hellenic demigod Heracles, who fought the giants and protected the gods during the Gigantomachy. We find similarities between this legend and the Ark of the Covenant. In the latter case, a golden chest housing the fragments of the Ten Commandments was imbued with supernatural powers and hidden in a holy temple (Mayor 2000).

for Troy, either lashed to the deck with ropes or placed below as ballast" (Mayor 2000, 105).

After a long sea voyage of nearly a week, Pelops's shoulder bone arrived at Troy, and just as the seer had predicted, the relic bore witness to the sacking of the city and the triumph of the Greek forces. Following their much-anticipated victory, the Greeks loaded the ancient artifact back on the ship and departed for Greece. However, the Greek vessel was met with a violent sea storm and was wrecked off the coast of Euboea. Their precious cargo was lost forever (Mayor 2000).

DEAD HEROES AND GIANTS FROM GREEK AND ROMAN MYTHOLOGY

"Across the narrow Dardanelles from Troy," Mayor writes, "the ancient Thracian Chersonese (the Gallipoli Peninsula) was the setting of a unique dialogue" (2000, 116). The work she refers to is *On Heroes,* written in about 218 CE by the sophist Philostratus of Lemnos. What is otherwise considered an early romance novel is also peppered with references to the discovery of cyclopean bones and enormous relics belonging to long-dead heroes and giants from Greek and Roman mythology.

The setting for the dialogue is the port city of Elaeus, at the mouth of the Hellespont. In the opening act, a rustic grape farmer turned philosopher and a merchant awaiting his trading vessel engage in intriguing conversation. The grape farmer tells the merchant he has heard rumors of gigantic bones being found, remains that supposedly belonged to giants and Greek heroes. He also claims to be well versed in the stories of men who had become Greek heroes during the Trojan War, such as Achilles and Ajax. The merchant then inquires about whether there is any "empirical proof" to support the belief in heroes who "averaged some 10.5 cubits in height (4.5 meters)" (Mayor 2000, 116). The farmer replies by listing some of the main heroes of Greek mythology whose bones had been supposedly found during the prior centuries, including

Orestes' 7-cubit skeleton seized by the Spartans from Tegea; Plato's account of a huge skeleton found by a shepherd in the aftermath of a massive earthquake in Lydia; and the unearthing of the giant Aryades on the banks of the Orontes. "The farmer's own grandfather," Mayor explains,

> had told him how the Roman emperor Hadrian came to pay homage to Ajax's relics after the skeleton with memorably big kneecaps was washed out by the sea just across the strait. Hadrian "embraced and kissed the bones and laid them out," apparently in the configuration of a man about 15 feet tall. Then the emperor built a fine tomb for Ajax's bones at Troy. . . .
>
> "Have *you* personally seen any heroes' bones?" asked the merchant.
>
> The farmer responded, "Less than fifty years ago, I myself sailed across the strait to Sigeum to view a vast skeleton that eroded out of a rocky cave on the cape." (Sigeum, near Rhoeteum, was the Greek hero Achilles traditional burial place.) . . .
>
> The upper body of the skeleton was concealed in a cave, but the rest of the bones extended some 10 meters onto the cape.* (Mayor 2000, 117)

Their appearance was distinctly human. According to the farmer, the cape had become a hub of intense activity at that time; immense crowds had gathered all around the Hellespont from across the Anatolian coast to as far south as Izmir. Speculation about the bones

---

*Such large bones indicate that something enormous once existed in that region, and it's possible that such remains were not of a gigantic human, but rather of a prehistoric creature. It's plausible that the region's inhabitants, unfamiliar with creatures of the Miocene epoch—an era of mammoths and other enormous beasts—or the even earlier periods of dinosaurs and massive reptiles, simply misinterpreted what they saw. However, the ancients who wrote down these records, as stated in the previous chapter, were far from ignorant savages and must have had a level of scientific knowledge comparable to or even surpassing our own.

was rampant. Finally, an oracle settled the matter. According to her, the remains were those of Achilles, making that the end of the story.

As the dialogue continues, the grape farmer tells the merchant that he and some friends sailed to Lemnos to view another giant skeleton discovered by Menecrates of Steira after an earthquake. "We saw that the bones were completely shaken out of their proper position. The backbone was in pieces and the ribs were wrenched away from the ver- tebrae. . . . As I examined the entire skeleton and the individual bones, I got an impression of terrifying size, impossible to describe" (Mayor 2000, 118).

The grape farmer then tells the merchant that during that very same year, "an enormous body appeared at Naulochus on the tiny island of Imbros (Imroz, Turkey), when a part of the southwestern promon- tory fell into the sea" (Mayor 2000, 119).

The grape farmer adds: "The broken-off chunk of earth carried the giant with it. If you don't believe me, we can sail there now—that skel- eton is still visible and it's a short trip" (Mayor 2000, 271).

To further validate his argument concerning the extinct colossi, the farmer instructs the merchant to sail to Kos, "where the daugh- ters of giants were buried," or to visit Phrygia to "see the giant Hyllos or Thessaly to see the bones of fallen giants" (Mayor 2000, 119). He also cites Mount Vesuvius as the place at which the Italians displayed the bones of giants slain by the gods of the Burning Fields (Phlegra), and mentions Olympia as a prime location where the monstrous bones of Geryon (a three-bodied, four-winged giant) could be viewed. Additionally, thousands of giants lay entombed beneath the soil of Pallene, in northern Greece, "where thunderstorms and earthquakes expose their colossal bones on the surface of the ground" (Mayor 2000, 119).

The farmer concludes his saga with a blood-drenched account of a battle that had taken place during the Trojan War. He describes how Achilles' carnivorous warhorses slaughtered the Amazons, the mighty female warriors, and scattered their crushed limbs on the island of Leuke (in the Black Sea north of the Danube).

Thus, Philostratus's dialogue ends.

This is an intriguing story, and there is much to be gleaned from it with regard to the ancients' fascination with giant bones—a phenomenon seen all the way to modern times, as we shall read about shortly. Before so doing, however, we will explore how a cosmology that included the existence of giants would have been reflected in the larger worldview of Greek and Roman philosophy and scientific thought.

ANCIENT PALEONTOLOGY IN WRITTEN WORKS

Mayor continues by presenting the story of some of the earliest fossil evidence for giants, monsters, and other fantastic creatures. As well, she makes note of gaps in the ancients' accounts when discussing the truth about giants and the amateur's drive to expose it.

Mayor writes:

> Scholars both ancient and modern consigned descriptions of giants and monsters to the realm of fantasy and superstition. Since discussions of remarkable remains are missing in the "objective" writings of the best-known classical historians, like Thucydides, and natural philosophers such as Aristotle, most modern historians and scientists have simply assumed that large prehistoric remains went unnoticed in antiquity. . . . The empirical experiences narrated by travelers, mythographers, ethnographers, geographers, natural historians, compilers of natural wonders, and other hard-to-classify ancient writers tell a very different story—a story confirmed by archaeological evidence. (Mayor 2000, 4)

The world of ancient paleontology is preserved in these ancient written works. In the fourth century BCE, the philosopher Plato makes an allusion to giant-sized bones in *The Republic,* the only reference ever made by Plato regarding remarkable humanlike remains. He refers to folklore about Gyges, a seventh-century BCE tyrant of Lydia, who lived in present-day Asia Minor. According to Mayor, Plato explains "a violent storm and an earthquake broke open the ground, revealing a hollow bronze horse containing a gigantic skeleton and a magic ring" (Mayor 2000, 193). Because Plato often manipulated folk genres for his own purposes, we can't know whether he was citing actual lore, but the anecdote does capture the texture of later reports of large fossil discoveries by Pausanias and others (Mayor 2000).

Skeptics would readily dismiss such tales as balderdash. However, as the Greek philosopher Strabo observes, even for those who normally consider such stories as myths and nothing more, they are still worth further study "since the ancients expressed physical notions [and] facts enigmatically . . . and added the mythical element to their accounts. It is not easy to solve with accuracy all the enigmas, but if one studies the whole array of myths, some agreeing and others contradictory, one might be able to conjecture the truth" (Mayor 2000, 194).

HOW THE CONCEPT OF THE GIANT IMPACTED GREEK THINKING

For the Greeks and Romans of the classical era, all living things were spiraling downward to oblivion, their vigor sapped by the passing of ages. The Earth's energy was forever diminishing, and its life-producing powers were severely weakening. This was seen to be the eternal order of all life. This viewpoint, Mayor argues, was deduced by the ancestors from the fact that fossil skeletons from the ancient past were notably more massive by far than any of the humans or animals from their own time (Mayor 2000).

In classical antiquity the typical height for a healthy adult male was about five feet five inches tall. On the other hand, the traditional height for a mythical hero exceeded well over fifteen feet. When great bones were discovered, it was widely concluded that they were relics from the epoch when the Earth was young. Upon witnessing a group of such bones being excavated in a township not far from the Bay of Naples, the historian Pliny declared: "It is obvious that the whole human race is becoming shorter day by day!" A statement such as Pliny's is consistent with the intuitive idea of biological "decline." Indeed, examples in the ancient Greek and Roman's own recent history show how the wild cattle of the Bronze Age were significantly more imposing than the domesticated farming cattle of their own time. Furthermore, had it not been written in the ancient scriptures that the great heroes of antiquity pursued larger game than were available today?

However, in actual fact, Mayor explains: "Gigantism usually does fail to maintain viability: the most titanic prehistoric faunas did die out or evolved into smaller forms. And in some Mediterranean islands, the largest species, mammoths and hippos, tended to become smaller over time, while certain tiny species, like mice, grew bigger, as though striving for some Aristotelian mean" (Mayor 2000, 318).

This viability factor, however, does not discount the fact that giants could and did exist. "Who else but supersize men," Mayor asks, "could have piled massive boulders into the Bronze Age fortifications—already unthinkably ancient by the classical era—known as Cyclopean (Cyclops-built) walls?" Even Thucydides, a fifth-century historian and general skeptic, admitted that there was some truth to accounts of giants. In fact, he has become our initial source for placing two prehistoric races of giants, the Cyclopes and Laestrygonians, in Sicily.

The Greeks and Romans were mindful that these prehistoric relics were more than mere curiosities and that they signified something vitally important to the preservation of their religious and cultural heritage. Instinctively, they knew by the "vast dimensions and worn condition of large, petrified bones . . . dark, mottled, disarticulated, fragmented" that they were artifacts of enormous antiquity (Mayor 2000, 202).

THE THEORY OF EVOLUTION AND THE CONCEPT OF EXTINCTION IN THE ANCIENT WORLD

How does the ancients' knowledge of the many ages of geologic time compare with ours in the present day? What did they believe about evolution?

In the pre-Christian era, it was generally accepted that change was the inevitable process of all life, and that animals and humans did in fact change over time. Indeed, in both Greco-Roman and early Hebrew mythic traditions, all species were not created at a single auspicious moment, but rather many new and exotic life-forms appeared and disappeared on a seeming evolutionary time line (Mayor 2000).

According to Mayor:

Extinction is a crucial concept in modern paleontology. It is generally assumed that the idea of extinction of whole groups of animals did not develop until the seventeenth century. But some 2,500 years ago, notions of extinction, both catastrophic and gradual, were developed by the Greeks and applied to remarkable fossil bones. The paleontological legend of the Neades of Samos clearly states that the huge remains belonged to real animals that had all died out before the first humans arrived on the island. Several authors placed the era of the long-vanished giants in the pre-human age when mountains were still being formed and the "origin of life was recent." (2000, 204)

Hesiod and Homer visualized a grand succession of new and unique specimens of plant and animal life bred by the gods and by nature over many generations. Such species antedated the emergence of modern humanity by many tens of thousands of years. Among these different species were creatures formed from the mating of different kinds of monsters. There were also the recognizable hybrids, such as the Centaurs, who featured the characteristics of both humans and horses. Additional examples include the Titans and the giants, who were known to have undergone their own process of biological evolution as they reproduced themselves over the centuries.

Thus, we see among the ancient Greeks and Romans the beginnings of a true understanding of the nature of descent by natural selection and ultimately both speciation and extinction. This can no doubt be applied to the giant phenomenon. As Paul Von Ward said at the beginning of this book, the existence of giants represents a forgotten, and hitherto disregarded, stage in the evolution of humankind. With that in mind, it transforms the search for the fossils of giants past and present.

The geomyths, or scientific allegories, of the ancient Greeks describe past epochs marked by the decimation and extinction of entire populations. These include many viable creatures. Among the noted geomyths is the Greek *Gigantomachy,* the narrative that sparked the genius within the classical mind to investigate further the possibility of locating the remains of their fallen heroes and giants. As Mayor asserts: "They knew that bones were all that remained of colossal creatures that appeared, reproduced, and then were destroyed long ago in specific locales where their skeletons were left petrified in the ground. Once the gods' Blitzkrieg ended the epoch of giants and monsters, those creatures were gone forever. The narrative closely parallels the modern concept of catastrophic extinction" (Mayor 2000, 205).

The concept of mass extinction of entire species prior to the emergence of modern humankind occurs throughout Greek mythology. One of the primary instruments of these extinctions was the Greek hero Heracles, known by the Romans as Hercules. According to myth, he destroyed the Centaurs and exterminated the native population of large predators in Crete and North Africa. He also killed all the remaining sea monsters in the Mediterranean.

Orion, a giant son of the Earth and the greatest hunter of all time, also wiped out many species of wild beasts and virtually obliterated the native fauna of the island of Chios. It was Orion's blind arrogance, however, in which he was prepared to exterminate every last animal on the face of the planet, that compelled the gods to destroy him and bury his giant carcass deep within the earth of Delos or Crete. Pliny recorded that on Crete an earthquake uncovered a huge skeleton, sixty-nine feet long, which "some people thought must be that of Orion" (Mayor 2000, 273).

THE "BONE RUSH"—THE QUEST FOR THE HEROES' REMAINS

During the seventh, sixth, and fifth centuries BCE, the entire Greek world experienced a "bone rush," as competing city-states searched for the bones of dead heroes and giants. According to Mayor: "Every city sought the 'peculiar glamour'—the religious anointment and political power—conferred by heroes' remains. The impressive bones were a vital physical link to the glorious past" (Mayor 2000, 112). We have to remember that in the Greek mythological tradition, heroes were always depicted as being of gigantic stature as an exemplification of their superhuman abilities and importance within the ancient Greek pantheon.

According to Mayor, Athens too was caught up in this archaeological fervor. The oracle at Delphi by this time had assumed a high level of importance in the search for these ancient relics. Indeed, her reputation as indispensable guide to finding bones had become widely regarded across the ancient world. The oracle instructed the Athenians that they could find on the island of Skyros the bones of their local hero Theseus, who the Athenians believed had been murdered and thrown off a cliff in the ninth century BCE. According to

Mayor, "the residents of Skyros," however, "denied the murder and refused to allow a search for his remains" (Mayor 2000, 112).

This problem was easily solved with military action. The Athenian general Kimon conquered the island, making the discovery of the sacred bones of Theseus his prime objective as governor of the new territory. Kimon noticed "an eagle tearing at a mound" and he gave the order to begin excavation at that site. Their digging revealed a number of massive bones lying beside a bronze-pointed spear and sword, typical of those used during the Bronze Age.

As Mayor explains: "Kimon loaded the bones and weapons onto his trireme and sailed back to Athens. Theseus's relics 'were welcomed with magnificent processions and interred in the heart of the city, and Kimon reaped many political points'" (Mayor 2000, 112). The discovery of these bones stands as significant evidence for the existence of beings of giant stature in ancient times.

Many of these ancient archaeological missions were recorded in ancient texts. Pausanias alone records over twenty-four such excavations at sites all over the ancient Greek world. During this "bone mania," the Spartans retrieved the remains of Orestes' son Tisamenus from the lost civilization of Helike on the Gulf of Corinth. In another example, the citizens of Olympia found and recovered the remains of Pelops's wife, Hippodamia. These relics were then installed in a shrine next to a mound that supposedly contained the bones of her father, "the giant son begotten by the god Ares upon the daughter of the giant Atlas" (Mayor 2000, 112).

To cure the onset of a disastrous plague that ravaged the community of Orchomenus in the region of Boeotia in the fifth century BCE, the oracle revealed that the remains of the religious writer Hesiod* could and should be located. According to myth, a raven scratched at a hollow

---

*Hesiod's main contribution to Greek religion, the *Theogony,* was widely considered by the ancient Greeks to be divinely inspired, and it was viewed as a sacred text comparable to the Book of Genesis in the Old Testament.

mound, after which a number of large bones spilled out. The remains were retrieved and reburied in an agora, an ancient temple.

The difference between these ancient archaeological missions and those of today is clear. The ancients undertook excavations largely to win wars or to cure plagues, or to ensure the well-being of a nation, not to obtain a richer understanding about the nature of ancient cultures and civilization or to determine how society had changed over time.

DID ANCIENT ARCHAEOLOGISTS KNOW WHAT THEY WERE FINDING?

Clearly our ancient ancestors believed in the myths and legends that articulated the existence of giants in their remote past. From this essential belief, they then began identifying all cyclopean remains as belonging to an extinct race of giants. How firmly grounded in reality were such assertions? Could ancient peoples discern the difference between the remains or fossilized bones of an extinct animal and those of a human or humanlike giant?

Mayor points out that: "People of antiquity were well acquainted with animal and human anatomy. Hunting and butchering animals, animal sacrifices, and ritual cremation and inhumation of the bones of their dead made skeletons very familiar objects. Evidence from Herodotus shows the ancients' deep interest in examining any bones they came across for unusual features" (Mayor 2000, 199). Thus it would appear that ancient humans *did* have the knowledge necessary to distinguish between animal and human or humanlike remains. Inevitably, this leads us to one conclusion: Ancient giants were in fact being uncovered by the ancient Greeks and Romans, and quite possibly by earlier cultures.

Indeed, as Mayor asserts, the renowned fifth-century BCE Greek historian Herodotus himself went on many investigations to exhume and examine the bones of the dead. In 440 BCE, for example,

Herodotus visited a former battlefield to undertake a study of human remains at the site. This battlefield marked the victory of the Persians over the Egyptians in 522 BCE. The sun-bleached skeletons littered the ground on which they fought and perished. Wandering about the site, examining the fleshless corpses, Herodotus studied the differences between the skulls of the two races. He then cataloged and documented these differences. These were the first stirrings of scientific anthropology, nearly 2,500 years before the formal scientific discipline was invented and defined.

At yet another location, this time in Boeotia in central Greece (then part of ancient Greece), Herodotus reported the discovery of a seamless skull, a bizarre jawbone, and a 7.5-foot skeleton. These finds were unearthed four years after the battle of Plataea, in 479 BCE. Citizens found the bones while scavenging the battlefield for sacred relics, for it was common practice for the average person to mine the sites of great battlefields in this manner. The objective was to find something that could be used for a magical talisman or even a valuable object for scientific investigation. Often very little would be left after the masses had their way. "Such accounts [those of Herodotus for instance]," writes Mayor, "reveal the ancient fascination with examining, comparing, and measuring human and/or remarkable bones" (Mayor 2000, 199). These early excavations can be said to represent the roots of modern archaeology.

ORESTES AND HIS SACRED REMAINS

According to Herodotus, an intense rivalry among the early Greeks— to gather together the various sacred bones and holy relics of the classical world—ultimately led to Spartan military dominance within the Peloponnese. In 560 BCE, the oracle at Delphi told the Spartans that if they wanted to successfully overcome their chief adversaries, the Arcadian Tegea, they would have to locate the sacred remains of the hero Orestes.

However, there was one problem: The Spartans had no clue where the tomb of Orestes lay. They returned to Delphi and requested that the oracle give them precise directions to the tomb. In response, they were given a cryptic verse about a forge and its blacksmith. The key to discovering Orestes, the oracle insisted, could be found only when the forge was finally located. These words dumbfounded the eager Spartans, who felt betrayed by their own oracle. But this misfortune was soon to be transformed (Mayor 2000).

While traveling through Tegean territory, a retired Spartan cavalryman, Lichas, encountered a blacksmith working at his forge. Lichas approached the blacksmith and greeted him, striking up a conversation. The blacksmith then guided Lichas to his yard. The smith then told Lichas that more than a year before, he had been digging his well when his spade struck something hard. It was then that he came upon an awesome discovery: a huge coffin some seven cubits long (three meters) was buried in the earth. He opened the lid of the casket and found the skeleton of a giant, also seven cubits long. At that moment Lichas realized he had found the tomb of Orestes.

Lichas pretended to be an exile from Sparta and asked the blacksmith if he could rent a room in his home for the night. The blacksmith agreed. During the night, Lichas snuck out into the yard, dug up the bones, and took them back to his fellow Spartans. As soon as they were in possession of this sacred talisman, the Spartans took control of the Peloponnese and became the dominant power in the region. The city trumpeted Lichas's victory, and the bones were afterward buried with much pomp and ceremony (Mayor 2000).

THE *GIGANTOMACHY* AND GIANT FOSSIL DISCOVERIES

Another account links events in an ancient Greek myth to actual fossil beds in which giants' remains were alleged to have been found. Herein lies the tale: Once the battle between the Titans and the more human-like Olympians came to a close—as depicted in the *Titanomachy*—yet another battle loomed on the horizon. This time the more monstrous giants such as Typhon would be pitted against the Olympians and their champion Heracles. This great battle was recorded in the Greek myth the *Gigantomachy*.

According to Mayor, "Zeus, hurling his bolts of thunder and lightning, destroyed legions of giants and Typhon. Heracles killed numerous giants and monsters, including Geryon, while the other gods, goddesses, and heroes and heroines slew still more giants and monsters all around the Mediterranean. The defeated giants and monsters were buried in the earth where they fell" (2000, 195).

Gigantic humanoid remains were found in widespread fossil beds in ancient times, and it was conjectured that these were the bones of the fallen giants and monsters of the *Gigantomachy*. Mayor says, "Zeus slew armies of giants in Arcadia, Crete, and Rhodes, and the gods heaped the island of Kos on top of giants." All four places are now known to have yielded bones of giant humanoids, according to ancient historians such as Claudian (2000, 195–96). Mayor also mentions that: "An eroding cliff between Corinth and Megara was said to bear the petrified bones of the giant Skiron. According to myth, this ogre threw victims over the cliff to a monstrous turtle waiting below, until the hero Theseus threw him off the same precipice" (Mayor 2000, 196).

GIANTS COULD ALSO BE MONSTERS

Mayor also discusses the various forms that early giants could take: In early Greek art, giants were imagined as quadruped monsters, or as warriors, huge ogres, or primitive strongmen armed with tree trunks and boulders; some later artists added serpent legs to symbolize their earthborn nature. It's important to keep in mind that giants were not necessarily visualized as human. In the words of Manilius (first century BCE), the giants were broods of "deformed creatures of unnatural face and shape" that appeared and were destroyed in the era "when mountains were still being formed" (Mayor 2000, 196).

Mayor adds:

> Some giant monsters, such as Geryon and Typhon, and even giant heroes like Idas, were said to have multiple heads or an unusual number of limbs. This is a widespread folk motif denoting extraordinary strength. In the ancient Greek mythical metaphor, extra limbs and mixed animal-human features also indicated the composite nature of strange creatures whose bodies lay buried under the earth. (2000, 196)

These prehistoric creatures, far from being recognizable by mainstream paleontologists as mastodons or dinosaurs, are in fact beasts of unexplainable origin.

Mayor continues:

> Zeus's cosmic lightning decisively ended the age of giants and monsters, and a new epoch began. The carcasses of the defeated creatures ended up in the ground all around the Mediterranean world, where they were later revealed by natural forces or human digging. The possession of such links to the mythical past became in many places a matter of local pride.
>
> For example, Anatolian Lydia, Spanish Cadiz, Thebes, and Olympia each claimed to have the body of Geryon, and the huge oxen were said to have been dispersed around mainland Greece (Arcadia, Attica, Epirus), in Italy, in Asia Minor, and on the shores of the Black Sea. Typhon's lightning-blasted corpse was variously thought to the buried in Syria, Cilicia (southern Turkey), Phrygia (north-central Turkey), and Sicily. The ancients identified sites

notable for their concentrations of enormous bones as major battlefields of the *Gigantomachy*. In Arcadia, Pausanias visited places
where the battles supposedly raged, around Megalopolis, Trapezus
(Bathos), and Tegea where the giants had made their last stand.
(Mayor 2000, 197)

As described earlier, Pallene, also known as Phlegra, was considered the homeland of the giants during the great battle depicted in
the *Gigantomachy,* their very own Atlantis reborn from the ashes of
destruction to serve their needs and their needs alone. A number of
ancient writers referred to the continual exposure of gigantic bones
around the mountainous island of Phlegra. Many more fallen giants
were located in the Bay of Naples and in southern Spain around
Tartessos.

In 1902, Professor Theodore Skoufos, a famed Greek paleontologist, excavated along the banks of the Alpheios River in search
of Pleistocene mammoth remains. This yielded little evidence of
Pleistocene mammoths, but did produce several anomalous pieces of
bone that remain unidentified to this day. It was at this very location that Pausanias conversed with locals about the possibility that
that area was, in fact, made up of suspected Gigantomachy battle-
grounds. The Arcadians, he learned, "sacrificed to violent thunder
and lightning storms" at Trapezus, where, according to Mayor, "the
ground still smolders. . . . They say that the legendary battle of gods
and giants took place here, and not at Thracian Pallene [the giants'
legendary headquarters in Chalkidiki]" (Mayor 2000, 198). Appian,
a contemporary of Pausanias, recounts that lightning was also worshipped in Syria, where Zeus's mighty thunderbolts bested the giant-
beast Typhon, and where the earth still burns.

Indeed, there is a widespread mythological tradition in classical
antiquity of monsters and giants being thwarted by lightning bolts
hurled by the gods. One can see this even in Norse tradition, in which

Thor's hammer emits bolts of lightning when he battles the frost giants, killing some, maiming others. The "lightning bones" gathered traditionally in the Siwalik Hills in the northwestern region of the Indian subcontinent provide another example. In a North American account, in the South Dakota badlands American Sioux Indians claimed to have discovered the bones of lightning-struck "thunder beasts" and various giants of Sioux legend.

Interpreting a metaphorical connection between lightning storms and the discovery of giant-sized humanoid fossils, Mayor concludes by saying: "The lightning motif reflects the natural fact that violent thunderstorms expose big fossils to view, but it also reflects the attempt to imagine a force powerful enough to destroy monsters of such size and strength" (2000, 198).

HERCULES AND THE BODY
OF ANTAEUS

In Spain in 70 BCE, the Roman general Quintus Sertorius saw the tomb of Antaeus, the giant that had been killed by the mortal Hercules. According to Plutarch, the skeleton contained in the tomb measured six cubits in length (nine to eleven feet) (Wilkins 1952, 46). The Roman historian Plutarch further explains that it was Hercules who saved the entire pantheon by seeking sanctuary from heaven in Egypt to draw away the wrath of the abominable giants from Elysium. Ultimately, this is a myth that could quite possibly become euphemized as a war of insurrection against the Atlantean ruling class, launched with the aid of men of gigantic stature.

We have examined the ancients' fascination with what may have been the bones of the giants they idolized as heroes and gods. Now let's examine more recent findings, at the hands of archaeologists no less interested in their subject than were the ancients.

MODERN FOSSIL HUNTERS IN ANCIENT DACIA
AND THE DISCOVERY OF LONG-LOST TROY

The year was 1843 in a tiny Moldavian village in ancient Dacia, northwest of the Black Sea. Peasant farmers plowing their fields unearthed a series of enormous remains. One find was an upright giant. The simple villagers who "flocked from all over, singing and dancing" around the remains thought that the bones of a dead saint had been restored to life, though the records do not indicate which saint it supposedly was. The military governor at the time, however, maintained that the bones were the remains of a Roman soldier of unusually gigantic stature (Mayor 2000).

In the same century, a German businessman turned archaeologist, Heinrich Schliemann, found the remains of the fabled Troy of yore, which for centuries was considered to be mythical, akin to the lost civilization of Atlantis in many skeptics' minds. There was no real effort to investigate it, because the assumption was that there was nothing to be found. In the early 1870s, however, that view was to change forever.

Schliemann decided to prove once and for all that the age of Greek heroes as described in the works of Homer and Virgil were in fact based on factual historical events. He immersed himself in the stories of the Greek hero Achilles, his king, Agamemnon, and the steadfast Odysseus, whose perilous journey homeward has become an ideal resource in understanding the Greek version of the giant mythos.

In April 1870, Schliemann commenced excavations at the site of Hissarlik in western Turkey. By 1871, Schliemann's team discovered the remains of a city that perfectly fit Homer's description of Troy. But not only did he find *one* Troy, he found nine successive layers of ruins dating to pre-Homeric times. Schliemann identified the sixth layer as the historical Troy, but today another layer, labeled Troy VIIa, is considered the actual site. It dates from the Late Bronze Age, and in 1220 BCE it withstood a prolonged siege—just as described in Homer's *Iliad*.

In this chapter we have covered a good deal of important ground and gleaned many insights concerning the prism through which the ancients of the classical world viewed giants, and how the idea of giants fits into their overall cosmology. In the chapter ahead we will cast our gaze to the north and west of Europe in an attempt to determine how the people of old who inhabited that unique landscape viewed giants.

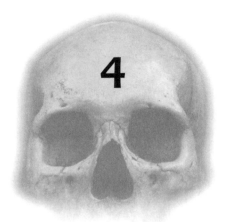

CLASH OF THE GODS

The Norse Deities and Giants

From a realm of cold and darkness came the frost giants,
threatening to plunge the mortal world into a new ice
age. But humanity would not face this threat alone. Our
armies drove the frost giants back into the heart of their
own world. The cost was great. In the end, their king fell.
And the source of their power was taken from them. With
the last great war ended, we withdrew from the other
worlds and returned home to the realm eternal, Asgard.
And here we remain as the beacon of hope. Shining out
across the stars. And though we have fallen into man's
myths and legends, it was Asgard and its warriors that
brought peace to the universe.

ODIN, THE ALL-FATHER: *THOR* (2011 FILM)

A WORLD OF SNOW MONSTERS
AND FROST GIANTS

The early beliefs of Northern Europe encompass a rich and sinister mythological tradition that includes not only giants, but an entire host of magical and mystical creatures. The ancient Norse divided the peoples of the world into three distinct categories: civilized people; barbarians, such as the Nordic peoples themselves; and subhumans, such as the *skraelings,* or native peoples of North America. When the Vikings entered a region for the first time, they took their swords and battle axes in hand and tested them out on anyone they encountered, to determine whether they could be killed and thus were human or whether they were invincible, which meant they were giants or members of one of the other many magical races, and therefore immortal. Examples of the magical races include orcs, trolls, elves, half gods, and, of course, giants. All of these were very similar to the creatures that the famous author J. R. R. Tolkien wrote about in *The Hobbit* and *The Lord of the Rings.*

In attempting to understand the Norse mythology, we need to understand its origins. According to late-nineteenth- and early-twentieth-century writer Donald A. Mackenzie, Celtic and Teutonic (Norse) mythology demonstrate a definite commonality. "It would appear," he writes:

> that archaic giant-lore is pre-Celtic and pre-Teutonic, and therefore implies a common inheritance. In the wars of the Olympians and Titans, of the Irish Danann gods and the Fomorachs, and of the Aesir and the Jotuns, we may have echoes of ancient racial conflicts. The old tribal peoples attributed successes to their gods, and remembered their battles as the battles of rival gods. For these giants are also gods of archaic conception. In Scotland, certain of them are associated with the fortunes of families and tribes. On the other

hand, gods are but exalted giants; the boisterous Olympians find their counterpart in the boisterous Scandinavian Jotuns rather than in the more refined Aesir and Vanir. (Mackenzie 1912)

Odin, the king of the Norse gods and the Germanic equivalent of Jupiter, is in reality a one-eyed giant, a Cyclops; his eye was sacrificed to Mimir's pool to obtain the Jotuns' gift of divine prediction. Odin is also described as the wind god, or the Wild Huntsman. Odin's son, Thor, was originally an oak god. The sacred tree of Odin in northern Germany was a one-thousand-year-old oak at the time of its destruction by Christian forces.

THE WARLIKE NATURE OF EARLY NORSE GIANTS

The heroes of the Teutonic culture were fierce in their determination not to be outdone by all manner of giants that they frequently fought against. Mackenzie writes: "When the tribal heroes of northern peoples were glorified by story-tellers, they were invariably depicted as giant-killers" (Mackenzie 1912). In *The History of the Kings of Britain,* Geoffrey of Monmouth describes the battle between the giant-killer Corineus and the most dreaded of all giants, the diabolical Goemagot:

At the beginning of the encounter, Corineus and the giant, standing, front to front, held each other strongly in their arms, and panted aloud for breath, but Goemagot presently grasping Corineus with all his might, broke three of his ribs, two on his right side and one on his left. At which Corineus, highly enraged, roused by his whole strength and snatching him upon his shoulders, ran with him, as fast as the weight would allow him, to the next shore, and there getting upon the top of the high rock, hurled down the savage monster into the sea; where falling on the sides of the craggy rocks, he was torn to pieces, and colored the waves with his blood. (Geoffrey and Thorpe 1966)

We see further examples of giant-slayers in the *Nibelungenlied,* with the mighty Aryan warrior Siegfried and Dietrich of Bern, in his Thunor character. Both are legendary and have become an integral part of Teutonic mythology and its modern interpretation. They are so inspiring that Richard Wagner successfully drew upon them in his pagan operas.

GIANTS IN THE EDDAS

In the Eddas, compiled by the Icelandic historian Snorri Sturluson in the thirteenth century CE, we are introduced to the only remaining accounts of ancient Teutonic mythology. These gory, blood-drenched tales of victory and conquest give us firsthand descriptions of the mighty frost giants. The giants are known by a variety of names, each of which had a particular meaning. *Jotun,* for example, means "the great eater," denoting their immense appetites, which corresponded to their enormous size. They were also described as being fond of drinking, so they were also called *Thurses,* a name that may be derived directly from the word *thirst.* (Some writers, however, attribute this name to the high towers—"turseis"—that the giants built on the mountaintops of Jotunheim [Guerber 1909].)

Two strains of giants are described in the Eddas: the children of Thrud and the children of Borr. The children of Thrud descend from the frost giant Ymir; the children of Borr include the Aesir, who are Nordic-looking and huge. These two divergent bloodlines would battle for supremacy over the cosmos for one billion years. However, both lineages can ultimately be traced back to that very first giant, Ymir, who was born in the Before-Time.

THE GERMANIC CREATION MYTH AND
THE BIRTH OF THE GIANTS

In his 1912 anthology, *Teutonic Myth and Legend,* Donald A. Mackenzie presents a provocative retelling of ancient German narratives. Recalling the earliest Norse accounts, he describes at length the initial events that sparked the creation of life; the birth of giants, gods, and humans; and the creation of the nine worlds. Mackenzie writes:

> In the Ages, when naught else was, there yawned in space a vast and empty gulf called Ginnunga-gap. Length it had, and breadth immeasurable, and there was depth beyond comprehension. No shore was there, nor cooling wave, for there was yet no sea, and the earth was not made nor the heavens above. There in the gulf was the beginning of things. There, time first dawned . . . northward of the gulf, Nifelheim, the immense home of misty darkness and freezing cold, and to the south, Muspelheim, the luminous home of warmth and of light. In the midst of Nifelheim burst forth the great fountain from whence all waters flow, and to which all waters return. It is named Hvergelmer, "the roaring cauldron", and from it surged, at the beginning, twelve tremendous rivers called Elivagar, that washed southwards toward the gulf. A vast distance they traversed from their source, and then the venom that was swept with them began to harden, as does dross pouring from a surface, until they congealed and became ice. Whereupon the rivers grew silent and ceased to move, and gigantic blocks of ice stood still. Vapor arose from the ice-venom and was frozen to rime; layer upon layer heaped up in fantastic forms one above another. That part of the gulf which lay northward was a region of horror and of strife. Heavy masses of black vapor enveloped the ice, and within were screaming whirlwinds that never ceased, and dismal banks of fleeting mist. But southward Muspelheim glowed with intense radiance.

Muspelheim is also associated with a great fire giant, Surtur, who possessed a flaming sword with which he guarded the gates to the realm of fire. Sparks, perhaps cast by Surtur's sword, penetrated the world of darkness and bitter cold. Drops of moisture then began to fall from the ice. Out of a frozen cocoon of hoarfrost and rime emerged the first being. Dark and formless, it eventually coalesced into something humanlike. At that moment the frost giant Ymir stood upright for the first time and surveyed his new domain. Ymir was called a *Hrim-thurs,* or ice giant, and was the personification of the frozen ocean (Guerber 1909).

When surveying his domain, Ymir caught sight of the bulging, voluptuous cow Audhumbla, licking her way through one of the many melting icebergs of hoarfrost and rime. Groping toward her, Ymir discovered the fresh, white milk flowing from her teats. Kneeling beside her, he gulped down the rich, frothy milk and allowed it to nourish and energize his body. He then wiped the hanging phlegm from his lips and emitted an echoing belch that reverberated throughout the ice field.

Audhumbla then continued to lick the thick blocks of rime around her, after which another being, Buri, a god, also known as "the producer," emerged from the ice. Buri was a fully formed deity, the first of his kind, according to Icelandic tradition. After the giant cow engaged Ymir, the mighty ice giant fell into a deep sleep. While he rested, a son and daughter were born from the sweat beneath his armpits. From his feet was born Thrud, the six-headed giant, who in turn birthed Bergelmir, the ancestor of all the subsequent frost giants. Buri produced a son named Borr, instantaneously, without the use of sexual reproduction, much the way Ymir produced his earliest descendants.

Once the giants became aware of the new deities' presence, they began to wage war against the gods. This became a protracted conflict with no end in sight—at least until Borr married the giantess Bestla, the giant Bolthorn's daughter. Bestla gave Borr three sons: Odin, Vili, and Ve, the first of the Aesir clan. Because Odin and the Aesir descended from the giant Bolthorn's daughter, it is quite clear that the gods themselves possessed the genetic makeup and physical appearance of giants in terms of size. To end the ongoing battle between the gods and the giants, Odin, Vili, and Ve hatched a grievous plot.

They ultimately decided to ambush Ymir and murder him. When they slit his throat, in yet another allusion to the Great Flood, a great deluge of blood rushed forth, which drowned most of the giants. Bergelmir and his wife escaped in a boat to found a new realm called Jotunheim. The world as we know it, Midgard, was formed from the body of Ymir. His salty, watery blood then became the oceans, rivers, and lakes; his flesh became the earth; his bones, the rocks and mountains; his hair, the forests; and the maggots from inside his stomach, the dwarves. When the first giant, Ymir, slumped down upon the icy ground, drowning his children in his blood, a series of events was set into motion that ultimately sealed the fate of the universe.

THE NORSE GOD THOR, KING OF THE PANTHEON

The ancient Nordic peoples believed that the giants were the first living beings to walk the primordial universe. In the words of historian H. A. Guerber: "These giants were from the very beginning the opponents and rivals of the gods, and as the latter were the personifications of all that is good and lovely, the former were representative of all that was ugly and evil" (1909). The giants were vulnerable to the gods because they were dimwitted and armed only with stone weapons for protection and assault. The Aesir, on the other hand, were fitted with bronze weaponry and armor. Despite this apparent inequality between the two warring camps, the gods often envied the giants for their mystical knowledge of the past.

The Norse god Thor is, of course, one of mythology's greatest warriors against the enemies of humanity—the dwarves, dragons, monsters, and, yes, giants. Bound by a solemn oath to protect mortals from the filth and treachery of giants, Thor was a fighting man, down in the trenches, battling for the fatherland and its people. The ancient Nordic peoples knew this; therefore, they proclaimed him the mightiest of all. His weapon of choice was a giant hammer, which according to Herbert Kuhn, a German scholar, means "stone."*

Thor's giant hammer, known as Mjollnir, like the Arthurian Excalibur, could penetrate any armor and shatter any sword. It also would return back to its master, whenever and wherever thrown, with magical swiftness. Thor's power belt increased his strength, and his iron gauntlets allowed him to wield his mighty hammer. Blazing across the grayish cloudscapes of the North Sea, he followed the retreating sun, known as Sol, on a chariot driven by two mountain goats called Tanngrisner and Tanngjost.

Thor represented a stronghold against the infamous frost giants, who were constantly at odds with both the Aesir and the Vanir. (In Norse Mythology the Vanir are a group of gods associated with fertility, wisdom, and the ability to see the future.) It is told by the wandering bards that on one occasion, Thor challenged Hrungnir of the giants to engage in single combat in order to settle long-held disputes. This was a common occurrence, even in the mortal world, in which Viking kings would settle their grievances by dueling instead of committing their sons to die in battle. Hrungnir and Thor thus gathered where the land of the Aesir and the giants met, and there the battle took place.

Fearful of Thor's growing strength and indomitable spirit, the giants built a cyclopean clay warrior called Mokkurkalfi. To animate the

---

*This association is the basis for a new theory linking the Iron Age god Thor to the Stone Age. Indeed, Herbert Kuhn has traced Thor back to the dimmest chapter in human history, the Old Stone Age, when hunter-gatherers living in caves dominated Northern Europe.

damned creation, he was given a mare's heart. Thjalfi, Thor's devoted servant, decided to stage a ruse prior to the upcoming battle. He told the giants that he wished to betray Thor and went on to tell them that Thor's attack on them would come from below. Thus, they braced for the attack by standing on their shields, but of course, Thor ploughed over them from above. He hurled his hammer, which split Hrungnir's skull. Bits of shattered bone showered over Thor and sharp pieces of it became lodged in his skull, which the witch Groa later removed (Grimm 1882, 429).

Thor was also the lord of thunder and rain and often carried a thunderbolt. In Sanskrit he is called Tanayitnu, or "the Thunderer" (Däniken 1970). Using his will, he manipulated every aspect of the weather, making him a favorite of sailors and merchants. With his mighty arm, he could throw magic and cast lightning.

He was married to the giantess Larnsaza, and from their fertile union two sons were born: Magni and Modi. Thor's second wife, Sif, bore him a son named Loride and a daughter named Thrud (Grimm 1882, 398).

During the Dark Ages, Thor and other pagan gods were gradually eclipsed by the followers of Christ, with Saint Boniface being a key figure in this regard. In the eighth century CE, the dedicated zealot Boniface was wandering through the forests of northern Germany when he came upon a horrifying scene: A group of heathen worshippers congregated around an oak, symbol of the Teutonic god Thor and his father Odin, as we have previously established. The heathens were preparing to sacrifice the son of their king, little Prince Asulf, hoping to ensure the well-being and continuation of their race. With one thundering blow of his bare fist, Boniface knocked down the tree. In its place grew a tiny evergreen, which, according to legend, became the first tannenbaum. This was the beginning of the end for Thor and his many adherents (Andrews 1974, 7–8).

EXPANDING PERSPECTIVES: FROM NORSE MOUNTAIN GIANTS TO SCOTTISH CAVE DWELLERS

In Hélène Adeline Guerber's classic work *Myths of the Norsemen: From the Eddas and Sagas* (1909), Guerber presents an intriguing story, one that explains the origin of Northern Europe's vast system of mountain ranges. Guerber writes that according to "German legends the uneven surface of the earth was due to the giants, who marred its smoothness by treading upon it while it was still soft and newly created, while streams were formed from the copious tears shed by the giantesses upon seeing the valleys made by their husbands' huge footprints."

Surprisingly, some Old Norse and German myths portraying the giants as the creators of Europe's great mountain ranges have survived to this day. Modern Icelanders have designated their highest peaks the *Jokul,* a modified version of the original Norwegian word *Jotun* ("the great eater"), and in Teutonic mythology, the giants were said to be hiding within mountain caverns amid the towering peaks.

The Swiss, a people who inhabit a land dominated by immense mountain peaks and everlasting snow, tell stories of ancient times when giants roamed the world. Indeed, they still identify the crashing of an avalanche down a mountainside with the shaking off of the ice and snow that accumulate on the heads and shoulders of ancient giants.

THE MYTH OF RAGNAROK

The Teutons developed myths concerning the end of the world, or "end-times" cosmology, which is very pronounced in the Christian tradition as well. In the Teutonic myths, the giants and their spawn—the Midgard Serpent—challenge the gods and humans for mastery of the universe. The main focal point of this last, great war, which ultimately will consume and destroy the entire universe and plunge the remnants of humanity into total darkness, is the battle between the forces of good and evil. In this battle, the gods who dwell in Asgard (the countryside surrounding Valhalla, the resting place of the slain) will fall to their death, and the world will be consumed by a maelstrom of steel and fire.

That sinister hour will be presaged by many terrifying omens. First, a bitter cold will descend upon the Earth, followed by a devastating winter that will last three unending and arduous years. The union of nations will be shattered, the bonds of kinship among humans will be demolished, and global warfare will break out as humankind commits insufferable acts of murder, rape, incest, and betrayal.

A giant wolf called Fenris, son of Loki (the Nordic god of evil, strife, and discord), will arrest the sun, causing it to grow dim and pale before he eventually swallows it whole. As Fenris advances further, he will gluttonize the moon and cause the stars to fall from the sky and crash to the Earth. Finally, with jaws agape, he will fill the gap between the firmament and the atmosphere. The mountains will collapse into fragments as the entire planet quakes and shudders in an immense bedlam of molten lava.

The Serpent of the World will soar from the sea, excreting poison upon the land, while Loki, bound and gagged for centuries, will break loose from his strangling chains and destroy everything, liberating hideous monsters from their shackles and commanding them to pillage the world. Naglfar, a boat made from the fingernails of the dead and navigated by Loki himself, will sail the oceans of the world, delivering wicked giants to distant regions and summoning the primordial waters to rise and flood the land (Davidson 1990, 26).

The fire giant Surt and his many adherents will rise from Muspelheim (a fiery realm between the Earth and sky that helped create the world) with blood axes and magical swords, pursuing their ultimate goal of attacking and killing the gods and goddesses of Asgard and Valhalla. Surt's forces will eventually join with the frost giants as they storm the Bifrost (the rainbow bridge connecting the Earth with the home of the gods) and cause it to disintegrate beneath the trampling hooves of their preternatural steeds. Then, as the giants storm the gates and the Twilight of the Gods looms imminent, the supernatural armies will meet on the great plain known as Vigrid. There the final battle between good and evil will transpire, and the gods will fall to their knees in a blaze of enormous intensity (Davidson 1990, 68).

All of these gods will die. Only Surt, the fire giant, will remain to burn the heavens and the Earth to ashes, and then he too will perish as the thrashing waters envelop the entire universe. Yet, beyond this traumatic catastrophe, hope rekindles: the offspring of the old gods shall remain alive, and Balder, the Germanic god of purity and justice, will be reincarnated and will reign with the remaining gods. With their assistance he will create a new race of divinities, to rule a newly purified and rejuvenated universe (Davidson 1990, 70).

The Earth will rise from the ashes—new, fresh, and fertile, more beautiful and more enduring than ever before. A man and a woman, having sought shelter from the holocaust in Yggdrasil, the World Tree, will subdue and repopulate the new world. They are Lif and Lifthraser, and according to author Frank Joseph, "Neither the sea nor Surt's fire had harmed them, and they dwell on the plains of Ida, where Asgaard was before" (2002, 127).

Christian monks wrote down this pagan story at a time when Christianity had been entrenched in the lands of the Norse for roughly three centuries, and indeed, Christian elements are reflected in it. For example, the two survivors represent the purely Nordic Adam and Eve, and as such, mark the beginning of a switch to monotheism and the end of the old Teutonic worldview with its many deities.

Now the cycle of creation had come full circle, for in the continuation of the story, a new sun, outshining its predecessor in radiance and beauty, was to travel across the azure sky, and the nightly heavens would be illuminated by a brilliance unlike any that humans have ever known.

This new universe, purged of treachery and corruption, will endure for all eternity (Davidson 1990, 78–80).

All of these Teutonic myths serve to help us better understand the ancient world in the Norse tradition, one peopled by giants and other creatures, as is consistent with the literature of cultures the world over. Given this consensus, it would be wise to pay attention to what the message is trying to tell us. In the next chapter we will explore accounts of giants in Africa and Australia, among others, in our ongoing attempt to determine the ultimate truth about this most compelling aspect of our collective past.

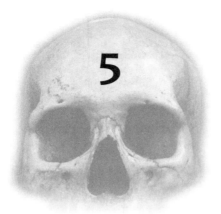

GIGANTOPITHECUS AND MEGANTHROPUS

African Giants, Australian Giants, and Giants of the Bible

In this chapter we will examine various accounts of giants from across the globe. We will begin with a discussion of an Asian hominid, *Gigantopithecus,* from which the Yeti—an early creature that was distinctly not *Homo sapiens*—may have descended. Another very large apelike human, linked to *Homo erectus* and known as *Meganthropus,* was found in Java in the 1900s and attracted the attention of the best paleontologists of the day, whose speculations we include here.

We next turn our attention to Africa, where intrepid explorers found the remains of giants in funerary jars in Chad; huge bones buried in a jungle in Central Africa that did not appear to be human in origin; a mummified ancient Egyptian 2.5 meters tall; very large weapons unearthed in Morocco; and a giant group of people from Sudan, called the *Nilot.* Following this, we cast our gaze down under to explore Australian reports—including some accounts of giant teeth—before opening the pages of the Bible to examine stories of giants contained therein, including the story of Goliath—that mighty monster of yesteryear.

GIGANTOPITHECUS AND MEGANTHROPUS

Evolutionary biologists have identified a giant humanoid race that they call *Gigantopithecus blacki,* standing 9.5 feet tall. Some believe that this creature may have been the ancestor of the Yeti, or Bigfoot. The colossal, manlike ape, which ruled the forests of East Asia and other parts of the world for about one million years, has been extinct for the past one hundred thousand years. The species coexisted with our immediate predecessor, *Homo erectus,* before our own species, *Homo sapiens,* made its appearance.

What we know of *Gigantopithecus* comes from the 1934 discovery of more than one thousand fossilized teeth by the Dutch paleontologist and geologist Dr. Gustav Heinrich Ralph von Koenigswald, who found the teeth in numerous areas throughout Southeast Asia. The Chinese, overlooking them as valuable pieces to our evolutionary puzzle, were selling these teeth (which they called "dragon bones") as cures for various illnesses. After World War II broke out in Europe in September of 1939, local Japanese authorities arrested Koenigswald as an enemy alien, thus ending his research. He was liberated in 1945, but much of his work had been destroyed in the conflict.

In their book *True Giants: Is* Gigantopithecus *Still Alive?* authors Mark A. Hall and Loren Coleman present their theory that "the living descendants of the fossil type known as *Gigantopithecus* might still be in existence," albeit in the New World, not in Asia (Hall and Coleman 2010, 119). They further explore anomalous archaeological finds and supposed bones of such giants that had been excavated—or were claimed to have been excavated—by an assortment of professional and amateur archaeologists. According to Hall and Coleman: "The record of giant bones from the New World can be grouped into three categories: (1) Bones recently found and lost; (2) Bones found early in this century [20th century] and in the 19th century; (3) Bones found centuries ago" (2010, 121).

They explain one find in detail from the second category:

> The lost bone most familiar to Sasquatch followers is likely to be one cited by John Green in *On the Track of the Sasquatch*. He learned from a woman in British Columbia how she and her husband had found some bones 20 years earlier (thus in the late 1950s). They were trapping near the Toba River at the time. . . . Over her husband's objections, she only brought out the jawbone; it was large enough to fit over her face. She kept it around the house and showed it to people for the next 10 years until the house burned down. (Hall and Coleman 2010, 121)

In another report, Dana and Ginger Lamb retrieved a complete skeleton of a giant from an Indian burial mound in Mexico. A smaller dwarflike skeleton accompanied it. The fingers on the giant's hands were twice the length of Dana's own. The Lambs assumed that floodwaters inundated and washed away much of the mound, thus exposing the bones for the first time in centuries (Hall and Coleman 2010, 122–23).

In addition to *Gigantopithecus,* yet another gigantic manlike ape appears in the fossil record, this time in Java. Individuals of this type are grouped under the umbrella genus *Meganthropus* and are considered by anthropologists to be a significantly larger form of *Homo erectus,* therefore linking the genus to more humanlike and subsequently more intelligent hominids.

From the beginning, *Meganthropus* was seen as a seminal find. Franz Weidenreich, an anthropologist from the American Museum of Natural

History, analyzed fossil remains that had been found throughout Asia. He wrote about them in his 1946 book *Apes, Giants, and Man.* In a chapter entitled "Giants as Earliest Ancestors," and referencing the noted German paleontologist and geologist G. H. R. von Koenigswald, mentioned above, Weidenreich writes:

> Early in 1941, I received a letter from von Koenigswald in which he announced the discovery of a fragment of another lower jaw, collected at the same site as the jaw found earlier (Sangiran). But this time the critical teeth were still in their place and showed only slight attrition. A sketch of the piece was added. Von Koenigswald wrote that its proportions are enormous. I asked for a cast. It arrived just a couple weeks after Pearl Harbor. It could be gathered from the label that von Koenigswald intended to give the new human type, represented by the gigantic jaw, the name *Meganthropus paleojavanicus,* which means "giant man from Java," and that he regarded the fragment as that of a male individual, which the fragment earlier, not yet recognized, was attributed by him to a female individual of the same type. (1946)

Weidenreich concludes his chapter by trying to place *Meganthropus* within a framework congruent with the known fossils of the 1940s:

> The only skull bone that challenges the Java jaw in massiveness is the jaw of Broom's *Paranthropus robustus* from southern Africa. This jaw belongs to that strange group of Australopithecines which shows the typical organization of anthropoids mixed with some human features. The species name, *robustus,* was given by Broom because of this extraordinary appearance of the jaw. The robustness of the *Pithecanthropus* skull is the link connecting it with the giant jaw from Java, in addition to the agreement in primitive human traits shown by both. This suggests that there

was a continuous line of gigantic and nearly gigantic human forms characterized by a gradual reduction in size, this reduction going hand in hand with a progressive trend in other features. For this reason I distinguish between the big *Pithecanthropus.* . . . The big skull apparently represents a special type already on the way to gigantism; therefore I gave it the name *"Pithecanthropus robustus."* (Weidenreich 1946)

Franz Weidenreich also makes the following observation, comparing *Gigantopithecus* and *Meganthropus:* "The molars of Gigantopithecus are more than one-third larger than those of Meganthropus, the Java giant, and almost twice as large as those of the big Pithecanthropus [*Homo erectus robustus*]" (1946).

Weidenreich's colleague von Koenigswald was to publish his own book on the issue of giant hominid evolution in 1962, entitled *The Evolution of Man*. In it he writes:

"Meganthropus had the largest human lower jaw so far discovered. It is roughly the size of a gorilla's (length of first molar: Meganthropus 14.5 mm; gorilla 15.5 mm; average Homo Sapiens 11.5 mm). [John] Robinson, who considers the jaw as that of Paranthropus, has shown that the two are comparable in size and structure" (Hall and Coleman 2010, 119).

Let's move on from these fascinating accounts to see what has turned up in Africa.

GIANTS ON THE DARK CONTINENT OF AFRICA

We find several key examples of giants on the Dark Continent of Africa. In 1936, French archaeologists Jean-Paul Lebeuf and G. Calame-Griaule launched an expedition into the north central African nation of Chad. While traversing the plains, they stumbled upon a number of ancient burial mounds. Additional burial mounds were located around

Fort Lamy and Goulfeil. The two archaeologists decided to excavate the burial site to determine who or what was interred there.

In addition to jewelry and artwork, they discovered several egg-shaped funeral jars containing the remains of an ancient race of gigantic stature. The archaeological team then questioned the natives. According to them, these giants were known to their people as the Saos. They had a "well-developed religion and culture"; they were fruitful and multiplied; and they established settlements at Fort Lamy, Mahaya, Midigue, and Goulfeil. They managed to avoid conflict, either internally or with neighboring tribes, but in the ninth century CE, the warhorse of Muslim expansion eventually brought an end to their centuries-long peace. The invading Arabs attempted to forcefully convert the Saos, and those who accepted the new Islamic faith lived in servitude and slavery to the Arabs. Those who refused were ultimately exterminated, with the upshot being that, by the end of the sixteenth century, the Saos had all but vanished from the face of the Earth.

In addition to the mysterious Saos, giants have been reported in the fossil record in Kigali Rwanda. These findings are a bit odder in that the creatures they reference may be of extraterrestrial origin. On June 24, 2011, the following article appeared in the Russian newspaper *Pravda:*

A team of anthropologists found gigantic creatures buried in the jungle near the city of Kigali Rwanda (Central Africa). The remains belong to gigantic creatures that bear little resemblance to humans. Head of research group believes that they could be visitors from another planet who died as a result of a catastrophe. According to the scientists, they were buried at least 500 years ago. At first, researchers thought that they came across the remains of ancient settlements, but no signs of human life have been found nearby. The 40 communal graves had approximately 200 bodies in them, all perfectly preserved. The creatures were tall—approximately 7 feet.

Their heads were disproportionately large and they had no mouth, nose or eyes. The anthropologists believe that the creatures were members of an alien landing, possibly destroyed by some terrestrial virus to which they had no immunity. However, no traces of the landing of the spacecraft or its fragments were discovered. (Troitsina 2011)

A cache of huge hunting weapons found in Morocco is another indication that giants once roamed the Dark Continent. Peter Kolosimo reports in *Timeless Earth* that at Agadir in Morocco, the French captain Lafanechere "discovered a complete arsenal of hunting weapons including five hundred double-edged axes weighing seventeen and a half pounds, i.e., twenty times as heavy as would be convenient for modern man. Apart from the question of weight, to handle the axe at all one would need to have hands of a size appropriate to a giant with a stature of at least 13 feet" (1973, 32).

Another example of African giants is not that of an extinct race, but a race that survives to this day, in the Sudan. Unfortunately, little has been written about this extraordinary people and yet we do have the brilliant and comprehensive work *Inside Africa,* by author and explorer John Gunther, that addresses the subject. In this seminal tome, Gunther names the race in question as the Nilot. According to him, they "have spread their virile blood far afield, as witness the Masai in Kenya and the giant Watusi in Ruanda-Urundi, who are cousins to the Hamitic Sudanese" (Gunther 1955).

The late professional basketball star Manute Bol is an ideal exemplar of this gigantic but very slender race of Dinka (the Dinka are derived from the Nilot). Bol was from the Sudanese region of Africa, where his height of seven feet seven inches was not an anomaly. According to the traditional creation myth of the Nilot people, in the beginning the universe was covered with sand and rock. Licking his way out of one salty block of rock came a giant, Binbali, who became the first living being. Then the sky people came and decided to divide Binbali's body into two parts and took his blood to form the rivers and lakes of northeastern Africa—including the Nile and the Indian Ocean to the east. The sky gods next took a primitive creature called Imzadi, raised him, and gave him super strength and height, making him the earliest member of the first race of giants, who were the ancestors of the Nilot.

Lesa, the most important of these ancient sky gods, came down to Earth to create the world. Lesa and the other sky gods were giants. They arrived on a shimmering cloud, and after they landed, they traveled east across the land. They created everything we now recognize as being part of the African landscape—rivers, hills, trees, grass, and sand. The sky people established the various nations and tribes of the Earth before traveling west and then back to the heavens. Lesa promised his children that he and the sky people would one day return. Before they left, as they walked across the Itabwa plain, they left their footprints in the mud. These footprints later hardened into stone and were preserved in solid rock. Called "the footprints of giants" due to their colossal size, they can be seen there to this very day.

The interesting aspect of this myth is how it contains elements of both the ancient astronaut theory and the ancient giant theory, and directly connects the two, proving that they are compatible.

THE TRUE GIANTS OF THE COMOROS ISLANDS

Located in the Mozambique Channel, four hundred kilometers east of the African continent, are the Comoros Islands. This ancient archipelago, volcanic in origin, hides one of the greatest secrets of the modern world—the presence of living giants. In 2005, Matthew Green of Reuters reported the islanders' belief in the Red Headband, a dangerous and powerful creature of giant-size stature:

Nobody has ever seen him and lived. Quite how the ancestors ever verified the existence of "Red Headband"—the Indian Ocean's answer to Big Foot, the Yeti and the Loch Ness Monster—is thus a mystery. What is clear is that when a volcano erupted on the largest island in the Comoros archipelago on April 17, an old story gained a new twist. Since time began, an evil spirit which appears as a giant human wearing his eponymous red headband has stalked the crater at the summit of Mount Karthala, sometimes appearing as tall as a house, or even, deceptively, as a dwarf. That's only when he's viewed from far away. "When people leave the village and they don't come back, we suspect they have seen Red Headband," said Ibrahim Ali, 60, a farmer from the mountain village of Idgikoundzi. . . . "Some people say they have seen him, and he looks like a giant," he said.

MYSTERIES OF THE ANCIENT AUSTRALIAN GIANTS

Moving from one part of the world to the next in our search for the remains of ancient giants, we now focus our attention on Australia and some archaeological finds that have surfaced there, specifically petroglyphs that are thousands of years old and as such, date to prehistory. They are depictions of four giant-sized figures with blue halos around their heads, their bodies fitted with long robes. Included with these images are inscriptions written in an unknown language.

While many adherents of the ancient astronaut theory consider them an early illustrated account of an extraterrestrial visitation, I think they might represent instead a forgotten race of giants. According to local Aboriginal belief, these drawings illustrate the first humans and were drawn by another race. The Aborigines also believe that both their own technology and their folk medicine derive from this single culture race, and posit that during the Dreamtime the first humans were beneficiaries of their immense power. There is nothing in this description, nor in the Aborigines' own words, that implies any kind of an extraterrestrial explanation.

One thing is certain: The Aborigines were not the first to reach Australia. Anthropologists maintain mainland Aborigines are in fact quite recent arrivals. Aborigines themselves acknowledge in their ancient folklore that this land was inhabited by several groups of humans, as well as giants, before they settled here.

Be this as it may, there also remains the strong possibility that these figures represent yet another distinct culture, perhaps travelers from the fabled continents of Atlantis or Lemuria, cultures highly advanced and of this world. The question is, of course, where did the Atlanteans and Lemurians get *their* technology?

Let's drill down a little deeper on the question of whether these figures represent ancient giants. Stephen Quayle touches upon the issue in his monumental undertaking *Giants: Master Builders of Prehistoric and Ancient Civilizations*. Regarding the possibility of giants in Australia, Quayle writes: "Because Australia has been settled only recently outside of the aboriginal tribes that have inhabited it for some time, not a lot of giants have been discovered on this vast continent. However, there are signs that giants walked this continent as well as other areas of the world, and some anthropologists have even gone so far as to suggest there was an entire race of such beings that should be classed as *meganthropus*" (2002, 308).

According to Quayle, in 1970 a number of gigantic fossilized footprints were discovered in Australia's Outback. This captured the attention of Dr. Rex Gilroy, director of the Mount York Natural History Museum at Mount Victoria, New South Wales. This finding was so significant and provocative that, after plaster casts of the footprints were made, Gilroy immediately started excavations in the Outback. Soon huge stone artifacts—clubs, pounders, adzes, chisels, knives, and hand axes—were uncovered "all of tremendous weight . . . scattered over a wide area. These weigh anything from 8, 10, 15, 21 and 25 pounds, implements which only men of tremendous proportions could possibly have made and used. Estimates for the actual size of these men range from 10 to 12 feet tall and over, weighing from 500–600 lbs" (Beckley 2009).

Gilroy became enamored with his quest and, throughout his career, attempted to prove his theory of the giant habitation of Australia. He was to continue to find ample evidence to establish that an ancient race of giants once dwelled on the Australian continent.

Another compelling find in Australia—that of a massive human molar—was uncovered by an archaeologist excavating the Winburndale River north of Bathurst. It was far too large to have belonged to modern *Homo sapiens*. An additional discovery was made near Dubbo, New South Wales, that closely parallel the tooth found at the Winburndale River. The Bathurst district also yielded a number of other intriguing finds. In the 1930s prospectors working there allegedly uncovered a number of large human footprints. They were found fossilized in shoals of red jasper.

Additional finds were also unearthed at Gympie, Queensland. A farmer named Keith Walker discovered the large fragment of the back portion of a jaw while plowing his field. The jaw still possessed a hollow cavity for a missing back molar. The owner of the tooth must have exceeded ten feet in height, a true giant by any means. The jaw and the discovered tooth later came into the possession of Rex Gilroy, the owner of the plaster footprint casts mentioned above (Beckley 2009).

In the Megalong Valley in the Blue Mountains of New South Wales, yet another phenomenal discovery was made. A large humanlike footprint was found in ironstone jutting from a creek bank. According to Beckley: "The print was that of the instep, with all 5 toes clearly shown. This footprint measures 7 inches across the toes. Had the footprint been complete it would have been at least 2 feet (60 cm in length, appropriate to a 12 foot human. However, the largest footprint found on the Blue Mountains must have belonged to a man 20 feet tall!)" (2009).

Beckley's compilation goes on to mention additional finds of this nature. "A set of 3 huge footprints was discovered near Mulgoa, south of Penrith, N.S.W. These prints, each measuring 2 ft. long and 7 inches across the toes, are 6 ft. apart, indicating the stride of the 12 ft. giant who left them. These prints were preserved by volcanic lava and ash flows which 'occurred millions of years' before man is supposed to have appeared on the Australian continent (if one is to believe the evolutionary theory)" (2009).

These last remaining relics of a forgotten age stand as a testament to a time when giants trod the Australian continent. However, in addition to the prevalence of these giants, Australia was also home to a number of ancient and sophisticated civilizations: some sources have proposed that the Egyptians, Celts, and Phoenicians may have been regular visitors to the southern continent.

Artifacts attesting to this have appeared in many areas throughout Australia, specifically, seventeen granite stones bearing confirmed Phoenician inscriptions. One reads: "The Eye of Ra the sun rule Sinim." Sinim is the Hebrew name for a mysterious southern continent described in the Old Testament. This land has also been associated with the Phoenician "Ofir," which was the source of King Solomon's gold. The Egyptians also referred to it as "the land of Punt." Other artifacts, seemingly Egyptian, have also been uncovered: In 1983, a "hand-made glass amulet" was found in the New South Wales town of Kyogle. It featured a stretched pyramid shape and Egyptian characters on four sides. A close comparison with other similar icons in Egypt and elsewhere led some experts to conclude that it must be at least five thousand years old.

Another intriguing anomaly was found on the Isle of New Caledonia, which lies approximately 1,210 kilometers east of Australia. Here archaeologists discovered four hundred anthill-shaped mounds of gravel and sand that they call tumuli. The mounds average eight feet in height and three hundred feet in diameter. As with the mysterious heads of Easter Island, archaeologists are unsure who built them or why. This mystery was only exacerbated by the discovery of upright pillars within a number of the tumuli. Current dating methods indicate that the pillars are between seven thousand and thirteen thousand years old, which engendered speculation from the lost continent and ancient alien theorists, who thought they were either landing beacons for alien spacecraft or the remnants of ancient temples dedicated to the gods of Lemuria or Mu. Academic archaeologists, meanwhile, continue to pursue explanations that better fit the established paradigm.

As the academics debate the vagaries of different facets of this discovery, local natives assert that the gods built the tumuli. Other locals even dare to mention a legend about a race of giants having created the tumuli and many other great monuments on their islands. Oceanic mythology (covering cultures from the Indian Ocean in the west to Easter Island in the east) is replete with references to giants and gods.

GIANTS IN THE BIBLE

The Bible is rich in giant symbolism and, as such, today remains one of the most authoritative works on the subject. In addition to the many pre-Christian Greek myths, the Bible lends credibility, even provability, to claims of the existence of giants.

The Book of Job is considered the oldest book in the Hebrew Bible. Job 26:5–6 reveals: "The primeval giants tremble imprisoned beneath the waters with their inhabitants. The unseen world [the bottom of the sea] lies open before them, and the place of destruction is uncovered." Author Frank Joseph links this description to an early reference to Atlantis. The giants here could be construed as being the original children of Atlantis, just as the founding fathers of Atlantis were a giant super-race known as the Titans, an earlier population of enormous gods that once ruled the primordial universe (Joseph 2005).

The Bible also describes what is perhaps the most famous giant encounter of all in Samuel 7:1–4: "And there went out a champion from the camp of the Philistines, named Goliath, whose height was six cubits and a span . . . and he was armed with a coat of mail; and the weight of the coat was five thousand shekels of brass and the staff of his spear was like a weaver's beam; and his spear's head weighed six hundred shekels of iron."

Goliath was the direct descendant of King Og of the Ammonites. Chronicles 20:3–8 gives a description of Goliath's lineage and how he came to confront David:

> And he brought out the people that were in it, and cut them with saws, and with harrows of iron and with axes. Even so dealt David with all the cities of the children of Ammon. And David and all the people return to Jerusalem. And it came to pass after this, that there arose war at Gezer with the Philistines at which time Sibbechai the Hushathite slew Sippai, that was of the children of the giant: and they were subdued. And there was war again with the Philistines; and Elhanan the son of Jair slew Lahmi the brother of Goliath the Gittite whose spear staff was like a weaver's beam. And yet again there was war at Gath [the legendary Philistine city and home of Goliath] where was a man of great stature, whose fingers and toes were four and twenty, six on each hand, and six on each foot and he also was the son of the giants. But when he defied Israel, Jonathan the son of Shimea David's brother slew him. These were born unto the giant in Gath; and they fell by the hand of David and by the hand of his servants.

Recently, a pottery shard was found in the ruins of Gath, dating to 950 BCE. It was inscribed with two non-Semitic names etymologically similar to the biblical name *Goliath*. Both names, "ALWT" (אולת) and "WLT" (ולת), were written in Semitic "Proto-Canaanite" letters. The dating of the artifact was consistent with the traditional biblical date as well. It is hoped this random discovery will lend credibility to the scriptural account (Maeir et al. 2008, 20).

In addition to the account of Goliath, the Bible contains more examples of giants, which should be mentioned here. In his book *Twilight of the Gods,* author Erich von Däniken devotes several pages to various biblical accounts of what may have been items belonging to ancient giants. For example, in the fifth book of the Pentateuch (Deuteronomy 3:11), the narrative speaks of a gigantic sarcophagus: "For only Og king of Bashan remained of the remnant of giants; behold, his bedstead was a bedstead of iron; it is not in Rabbath of the children of Ammon? Nine cubits was the length of it [about 8.5 feet], and four cubits the breadth of it, after the cubit of a man."

The farther we travel, the more evidence we gather; records of giants exist the world over. In this chapter we recounted more of them, including those found in the Bible, which provide scholars with some of the most culturally and religiously significant accounts of giants available in all the European and Near Eastern traditions. However, other accounts are linked not to the Judaeo-Christian culture, but rather to the diverse traditions of the New World. Let's set our sights on the Americas next, beginning with North America, before we move down to Central America, South America, and the ancient islands known today as Polynesia.

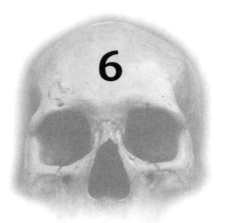

GIANTS OF ANCIENT NORTH AMERICA

Mainstream archaeologists hold to the basic tenets of the Clovis First theory with almost religious zeal. This theory is so-named for a specific type of arrow-point found in Clovis, New Mexico, during the early half of the last century, and considered by the establishment to be the Holy Grail of North American paleoarchaeology. In the estimation of these mainstream archaeologists, sporadic waves of migrations beginning around fifteen thousand years ago moved from Siberia across the Bering Strait and into Alaska. When an ice-free corridor opened up a few thousand years later, the Paleo-Indians, as they are called, roamed southward into virgin territory, soon to occupy the whole of the Americas. In their view, this established the Clovis people as the New World's first culture.

Many mainstream scientists now question this interpretation, but the number of academics who still cling to the old theory is truly staggering. As stated in previous chapters, ample evidence suggests that contrary to this view—that the New World was an unpopulated garden that became inhabited but a few short millennia ago—the New World is instead a land of vanished peoples and was the epicenter of a long-lost age of historical giants. Indeed, this evidence suggests that giants dominated the Americas for hundreds of thousands years before the arrival of Asian people from Siberia.

EARLY ACCOUNTS OF GIANTS BY EUROPEAN EXPLORERS

In their book *The Suppressed History of America,* Paul Schrag and Xaviant Haze write: "Meriwether Lewis, described as a giant of American history, may have been preceded by an entire race of real, historical giants" (2011, 90). Indeed, this, in short, summarizes the main thesis of the race of giants hypothesis on which this book is based. Throughout Schrag and Haze's work, they demonstrate how the famous American explorers and adventurers Lewis and Clark encountered stories among the Native Americans of a fallen race of giants. Furthermore, in many cases Lewis and Clark had their own close encounters with such beings. They wrote these down and then suppressed the accounts in later publications.

According to author Stephen Quayle, up until five centuries ago, the New World was still populated by living giants. Only in very recent times, the last few centuries, has evidence of living giants faded into the background. The only legends that persist are those of the mythical Sasquatch, which may or may not be a living species descended from *Gigantopithecus.* While the jury on that particular question is still out, let's look at a sixteenth-century account of the New World's giant phenomena.

In 1519, Spanish explorer Alonso Álvarez de Pineda mapped the entire Gulf Coast region, marking the various rivers and bays, noticeable landmarks and porting areas, all of which were the exclusive property of the king of Spain. After covering the entire coastlines of Florida and as far south as Tampico, Mexico, he returned up the Mississippi River, a journey he would never forget. Pineda was the first European ever to have ventured up the mouth of the Mississippi. He returned with an unbelievable account. According to Pineda, he found a large settlement of villages inhabited by giants. Pineda also claimed that these giants were friendly, and after some time he and his crew settled among them. There they rested, made repairs, and resupplied their foodstuffs, preparing for the journey onward (Schrag and Haze 2011, 91).

Pineda noted that there was an abundance of gold throughout the Mississippi and that the natives adorned themselves with gold jewelry and worshipped golden idols. Rather atypical for a Spaniard of his time, Pineda was less concerned with finding gold in the Mississippi and more captivated by the discovery of new lands and food, and the shock of finding a race of giants living among the native population.

After Pineda arrived back at his home base on the Caribbean island of Jamaica, he mentioned additional settlements of giants encountered on islands all the way up the Texas coast. He then presented Francisco de Garay, the Spanish governor of Jamaica, with his maps of the entire Gulf Coast along with his sketches and impressions of its inhabitants. These writings, archived by the famous Spanish compiler Martín Fernández de Navarrete, can be found by visiting the Archivo General de Indias in Seville, Spain (Schrag and Haze 2011, 92).

Twenty years later, the renowned Spanish explorer Francisco Coronado led an expedition across the American Southwest in search of the legendary Seven Cities of Cibola, known today as El Dorado. Throughout this quest, the expedition encountered numerous tribes of Indian giants. The man responsible for documenting these close encounters was Pedro de Castañeda, who traveled with Coronado and wrote firsthand accounts and histories of the expedition.

Castañeda's book describes this fascinating journey and discusses the adventures of a key crewmember, Hernando de Alarcón, regarding interactions with living giants among the North American Indians of the Southwest. Schrag and Haze explain the adventure:

Low on provisions, a frantic Coronado sent Alarcón to find a
river that could bring supplies more easily to the Spanish outposts
along the California and Mexican coasts. After nearly destroying
his ships and missing the waiting party at the rendezvous point,
Alarcón haphazardly floated up the mouth of the murky Colorado
River. Alarcón and his men became the first Europeans to fight
the rough rapids as he brought his fleet into the heart of the Colorado River, reaching as far as the lower reaches of the Grand Can-
yon. While coasting up the river, Alarcón and his men came upon
a settlement of an estimated two hundred giant warriors. These
giants, amazed by foreign intruders on the riverbanks, were ready
to attack.

Alarcón, however, averted conflict by offering them gifts and
entering in a peace treaty with the imposing natives. This quickly
diffused the situation and Alarcón and his fleet were permitted to
continue unmolested by the natives. These giants were later identified as belonging to the Cocopa Indians; even more of these giant
tribesmen were found further upstream. (2011, 92)

ORAL TRADITIONS OF GIANT
NATIVE AMERICANS

Oral traditions of most of the tribes of North America also contain
accounts of giants. Diné (Navajo) legends mention a race of "alien gods"
called the *anaye*. This name is also associated with a race that spoke
a distinctly non-Navajo language. These tremendous ogres towered
over the Navajo, "half as tall as the tallest pine-tree." They were distin-
guished as not being less intelligent than the Navajo and other Native
Americans, but also as being bloodthirsty cannibals who ravenously
devoured human flesh and even consumed one another.

Another giant, who bore the difficult name Tse'tahotsilta'li,
which means "He Who Kicks (People) Down the Cliff," was felled by

the Navajo cultural hero Nayenezgani ("Slayer of the Alien Gods"). Nayenezgani destroyed the wicked giant Tse'tahotsilta'li by hitting him right between the eyes with a stone knife. Tse'tahotsilta'li's twelve children then ravenously devoured huge chunks of their father's raw and bleeding corpse, while Nayenezgani went on the warpath and slaughtered eleven of these twelve children of the great giant. However, the final and eldest child was so filthy, ugly, and deformed that Nayenezgani took pity on him and spared his life. The boy giant, nothing more than a cannibal monster, traveled to Navajo Mountain (elevation 10,388 feet) on the Utah-Arizona border and, according to Native American legend, became the forerunner of the Paiutes.

ANCIENT GIANTS AND THE LIGHT-SKINNED PEOPLE

Some of the earliest surviving written and oral accounts tell of fierce, light-skinned peoples who were once the central force of a lost civilization. They claimed that their antecedents were a race of giants. In her book *To the American Indian,* Lucy Thompson writes:

> When the Indians first made their appearance on the Klamath river it was already inhabited by a white race of people known among us as the Wa-gas. These white people were found to inhabit the whole continent, and were a highly moral and civilized race. They heartily welcomed the Indians to their country and taught us all of their arts and sciences.
>
> The Indians recognized the rights of these ancient people as the first possessors of the soil and no difficulties ever arose between the two people. . . . Their morals were far superior to the white people of today, their ideals were high and inspired our people with greatness. After we had lived with these ancient people so long, they suddenly called their hosts together and mysteriously disappeared for a distant

land, we know not where. . . . Our people mourned their loss, as no more have we found such friends as they, so true and loyal.

In their farewell journey across this land they left landmarks of stone monuments, on the tops of high mountains and places commanding a view of the surrounding country. These land-marks we have kept in repair, down through the ages in loving remembrance. . . . When the Wa-gas left this land they assured my people that they would return to them at some future time. Perchance thousands of years have elapsed since then, and they have not returned, we have waited in vain for it seems that our cherished hopes are fading. However, some of our people are still looking for the return of the white man.

The traditions handed down leads us to believe that the Wa-gas returned to the land of their birth, in the far north, the valley of Cheek-cheek-alth, as their traditions were given to us that their origin was in this same land of Cheek-cheek-alth, as they came down from the North when they came to this land. When the Wa-gas first arrived on this continent they handed down the traditions to us that it was inhabited by a giant race of people when they first came.

These giants were represented by the Wa-gas as being very swarthy in complexion, and they used implements so large that no ordinary man could lift them. It was an age when large animals roamed the earth, and it seems the birds and fowls were all very large in size. It appeared to be the first age, and was the age of the giants. The recollections transmitted by the Wa-gas were that these giants were very cruel and wicked. It was said that God became displeased with them and destroyed them and they all perished from the earth.

It was also said that God appeared to the High Priest of the Wa-gas and told them that he was going to destroy the giant race and that the Wa-gas themselves would survive upon the earth as a new people. Smaller birds and animals would appear upon the earth for the use of man, thus the age of giants perished, but the Wa-gas do not hand down any tradition of how they perished from the earth, as my people have no recollections of ever seeing giants.

My mother says that our people in ancient times have seen many relics belonging to these prehistoric giants, such as huge stone bowls, stone slabs and other implements so great that our people could not move them. During the ages of rains and wearing away of the earth, these implements have been buried so deep and have sunk into the earth, is the reason we cannot find them today. The Indian name for the giant race is Pah-pel-ene, which means people that have all died and passed away.

When the Wa-gas returned to Cheek-cheek-alth it is supposed they found a ladder in this beautiful valley which extends from earth to Heaven, and climbed it to Werse-on-now, (Heaven) where they dwell with God. All the half castes with the exception of a few went away with the Wa-gas, and nearly all those that were three quarters Indian remained with our people. This is said to be the reason why some of our people are very fair. Some of the Indians are still looking for their return to the earth, when they come back it is believed that peace and happiness will reign supreme again over this great land and all evil will be cast out.

When the present race of the white people made their first appearance upon the American continent, we believed it was the Wa-gas returning and a hearty welcome was extended to them and there was great rejoicing among our tribes. But soon the sad mistake was discovered to our sorrow, when the men began to debauch our women, give whiskey to our men and claim our land that our fore-fathers had inhabited for so many thousands of years, yet not a single family has ever been driven from their house on the Klamath river up to this day. We no longer termed them as Wa-gas, but as Ken-e-yahs, which means foreigners, who had no right to the land and could never appreciate our kindness, for they were a very different people from the Wa-gas. They had corrupt morals that brought dissolution upon our people and wrought the horrors of untold havoc. (1916, 64–66)

ARCHAEOLOGICAL FINDINGS THAT SUPPORT THE LEGENDS

Indeed, the evidence for the existence of a superior race of giants in North America preceding the Bering Strait population from Siberia is striking. Sophisticated stone tools have been found in an ancient Mexican streambed. These artifacts were considerably more advanced than even those used by the European and Near Eastern populations thirty-five thousand to forty thousand years ago.

Dr. Ronald Frywell of Washington State University was quoted by Brad Steiger in his book *Worlds before Our Own* regarding these findings: "We have apparently found geological data that led to a head-on confrontation with apparently sound archaeological data." Steiger goes on to write: "People have been discovering data that simply will not fit into the accepted theories for the origin of the Amerindian no matter how much one bends, folds, or mutilates. How long these theories will be allowed to remain sacrosanct after such 'head-on confrontations' is a question that begs a forthright answer" (1978).

In reference to the monuments cited in Thompson's book about the Wa-gas, in addition to the incredibly ancient artifacts, some being as much as 250,000 years old, enormous walled cities and fortifications were found scattered across the United States. According to Steiger: "In Rockwall, Texas's smallest county, four square miles support the great stone walls of ancient fortification—some of which reach heights of forty-nine feet. The walls are about eight inches thick. The stones have been placed on top of each other with the ends breaking the center of the stone above or below, just as a fine mason would build a wall. The stones give the appearance of having been beveled around their edges" (1978).

There were also rumors of a vanished tribe that constructed an 885-foot wall on Fort Mountain in northern Georgia. The walls run east to west, and overshadow numerous pits or foxholes from which, it is imagined, defenders repelled invading armies.

Examples of massive stone walls and fortified cities in ancient America before the arrival of Europeans could add to a renewed confidence in Native American ingenuity, but indigenous groups themselves maintain that these structures and artifacts are not products of their own engineering ability, but rather credit them to a race of giants known by a variety of names throughout the Americas and ancient Polynesia.

THE DISCOVERIES OF AARON WRIGHT IN 1800

At the dawn of the nineteenth century, a young settler named Aaron Wright chose a homestead situated on a large "mound builder" burial ground. There he unearthed the "Conneaut Giants"—the giant-sized, ancient inhabitants of Ashtabula County, Ohio. The discovery and the mounds themselves, which were found to contain unusual and enigmatic bones, were described in 1844 by Harvey Nettleton:

> The mounds that were situated in the eastern part of what is now the village of Conneaut and the extensive burying ground near the Presbyterian Church, appear to have had no connection with the burying places of the Indians. They doubtless refer to a more remote period and are the relics of an extinct race, of whom the Indians had no knowledge. These mounds were of comparatively small size, and of the same general character of those that are widely scattered over the country. What is most remarkable concerning them is that among the quantity of human bones they contain, there are found specimens belonging to men of large stature, and who must have been nearly allied to a race of giants. Skulls were taken from these

mounds, the cavities of which were of sufficient capacity to admit the head of an ordinary man, and jaw-bones that might be fitted on over the face with equal facility. The bones of the arms and lower limbs were of the same proportions, exhibiting ocular proof of the degeneracy of the human race since the period in which these men occupied the soil which we now inhabit.

William W. Williams's *History of Ashtabula County, Ohio,* published in 1878, is the first authoritative publication devoted to northeastern Ohio. In it are extensive accounts of various encounters with the gigantic remains of the "Conneaut Giants." For chapter 6, entitled, "The Mound-Builders," local antiquarian Stephen D. Peet provides the following detailed description:

An impenetrable mystery still hangs over . . . a race preceding the various tribes of Indians which history has come in contact with, and may be regarded as strictly pre-historic. . . . Ohio gives numerous evidences of such a race. Here, it would seem, was the chief seat of the ancient empire. . . . In this State two classes of works have been discovered. . . . [In] the southern counties the works are much more massive and distinct. They are also much more complicated and mysterious in their design. . . . The works at the north, on the other hand, are much simpler in their character, and are mainly indicative of a military race. Ashtabula County abounds in earthworks. . . . These works are generally situated on the banks of streams, or in such locations as to have attracted attention. . . . [Some] are works of defense, and are well chosen for this purpose. . . . That at Conneaut is situated on the summit of a lofty hill . . . which has been left by some former change of the bed of the stream. . . . A steep ascent protects it on all sides. The only approach is up a gradual slope to the eastward, formed by the narrow strip which has been left by the wash of the waters. The height of the eminence is . . . about seventy-five feet. . . . The only mark of artificial defense is found on the summit. This consists of a simple earth-wall built on the very edge of the bluff, and following closely the very line of the bluff. A ditch was on the inside of the wall, and the height of the wall may have been at one time five feet. Possibly a stockade may have surmounted it, making the inclosure doubly secure both from the natural and artificial defense.

The work has been described by those who visited it at an early date. The land thus inclosed was perfectly level, and embraced an area of about two acres, triangular in shape. . . . A single opening to the inclosure existed, and this was approached only from the level of the stream below by a narrow pathway. . . . The work might have served for a defense to the various tribes of Indians which inhabited the region, or it may have been the residence of the ancient people called the mound-builders. There is on the bank opposite this work, but farther down the stream, a large burial-mound, which might indicate that the occupants of this spot were of the more ancient race of original mound-builders.

This mound is beautifully situated on the very summit of the point of land where the river turns to the northward. . . . The location of this mound was favorable as a lookout, and connected with the defense. The defense itself might have served as a signal-station, to warn against the approach of an enemy from the lake below. There are also other mounds in this neighborhood, though they are of comparatively small size. They were situated in the eastern part of the village. It is not improbable that the Book of Mormon has some connection with these mounds, and possibly may have been suggested by them. Its author, Rev. Mr. Spalding, lived in Conneaut, and the story is based on the common sentiment that the descendants of the lost tribes buried their dead in large heaps, which caused the mounds so common in this country. Their arts and sciences and civilization account for all the curious antiquities found in North and South America. (1878, 17)

The Book of Mormon of the Church of Jesus Christ of Latter-day Saints has always been associated with myths and accounts of giants. Could it be that these mounds have something to do with this mysterious tome?

GIANTS OF THE NEW WORLD

Early nineteenth-century treasure hunters often dug into so-called "Indian mounds" of the American Midwest, hoping to find gold or precious jewels. Instead, they sometimes broke into ancient burials containing the skeletons of giants (Joseph 2013).

Often they couldn't believe that what they found might actually be giants' bones, and for nearly two hundred years, scientists rationalized that these oversized human remains only appeared as such because bones proportionately disarticulate in the soil over time. Beginning in the 1960s, however, improved excavation techniques and forensic procedures determined that the mounds' skeletal evidence did, in fact, belong to individuals of extraordinary stature. Even mainstream archaeologists came to admit that first-millennium BCE Americans, academically referred to as the "Adena," were at least *occasionally* given to physical height far above the modern average. Some of these specimens were seven feet two inches in length, although unofficial sources report other specimens being as long as eight feet.

None of this came as a surprise to Native American record keepers, who have long told of the *Ron-nong-weto-wanca,* or "fair-skinned giant sorcerers" that once strode across the American plains (Joseph 2013). We discussed these red-haired giants earlier in this book but bring them up again to underscore the point that they are more than an anomaly; they are a link to a forgotten race of Caucasian-like giants that once inhabited much of the New World.

Johann Friedrich Blumenbach (1752–1840) first used the term *Caucasian* in 1795 to describe the white population of Europe. He was a German physician, physiologist, and anthropologist, and one of the first scientists to study humankind as an aspect of natural history; his teachings in comparative anatomy were applied to the classification of human races. Blumenbach adopted the term *Caucasian* from native inhabitants of the Caucasus Mountains in southeastern Europe, a race he believed to be the most beautiful and vigorous on Earth.

Reports of ancient Caucasoid peoples thriving in remote corners of the world and then vanishing mysteriously from history have existed for centuries. These accounts speak of white-skinned, red-haired giants and yellow-haired barbarians in countries now almost exclusively populated by non-Caucasian peoples. In time, modern archaeologists found traces of the existence of these Caucasoid peoples: millennia-old corpses preserved in desert sands or frigid glaciers were unearthed.

In addition to such physical remains, a wealth of historical and mythological evidence both in written form and oral tradition spoke of lost civilizations consisting of fair-skinned gods and light-eyed benefactors who helped to establish new cultures. According to numerous Native American accounts, at the dawn of their society they were visited by a Great White God arriving from a faraway land located across the sea. He helped them to establish their new mode of life and then departed, promising to return someday.

The discovery of light-skinned mummies in New Guinea and New Zealand, along with persistent references to godlike, light-skinned peoples inhabiting a now-sunken landmass in the Pacific Ocean, has upped the ante on this supposition. In the last decades of the twentieth century in particular we saw a revolution in our understanding of the magnitude of prehistoric Caucasian migration and influence.

In 1959, hard, physical evidence of proto-Caucasoid peoples existing in the Americas during prehistory began to surface. Archaeologists digging on Santa Rosa Island, off the California coast, unearthed a number of skeletal remains—having apparent Caucasian features—dating to 10,000 BCE. During the sixteenth century, as Spanish explorer Juan Rodriguez Cabrillo skimmed the same coastline, he found that native Chumash Indians possessed physical attributes that set them apart from the rest of the Channel Island Indians. He reported that the women had "fine forms, beautiful eyes, and a modest demeanor," and their children were "white, with light hair, and ruddy cheeks."

Also in the New World, the 1990s saw the discovery of the most controversial archaeological find in North American history: Kennewick Man, a nine-thousand-year-old Native American with clearly Caucasian, not Asian, traits. Additional discoveries throughout the Americas hint at a primordial Caucasoid population that roamed freely across much of the Western Hemisphere.

In March 2010, the archaeological community was stunned by the discovery of yet another Caucasian skeleton, this time in Mongolia. DNA extracted from this individual's bones confirmed a direct genetic link to the West. In essence, these remains were clearly European. This time, however, the ancient corpse was not as old, dating to the first century CE. Judging by the artifacts found at the burial site, the Mongolian individual was apparently held in high regard by his peers and seemed to have been a prominent figure in the Xiongnu Empire, a multiethnic melting pot of former Eurasian nomads who challenged the Han Dynasty supremacy. This ancient conglomeration of foreign tongues and non-Asian races no doubt consisted of many Indo-European-speaking peoples.

In Peru in 2007, Peruvian investigators found literally dozens of Caucasian mummies in a vaulted tomb buried eighty-two feet beneath the forest floor of the Amazon jungle. These belong to a pre-Inca race known as the *Chachapoyas,* or "Cloud People." Their discovery complements sixteenth-century Spanish reports of "strange, white Indians" with beards, found in the same region.

Even the giant statues of Easter Island, 2,180 miles off the Chilean coast, bear witness to the arrival and passage of an ancient Caucasoid race. In 1915, British archaeologist Katherine Routledge learned from a native islander the true nature of the Long Ears:

> men who came from far away in ships. They saw they had pink cheeks, and they said they were gods. The last real *ariki,* or chief, was said to be quite white. "White like me?" I innocently asked.
>
> "You!" they said, "you are red," the color in European cheeks. (221)

Red is "the term generally applied by Easter Islanders to Europeans. And *urukeku* is often translated 'red-haired.'" Indeed, the towering statues obviously displayed something other than Polynesian physiognomy, "and if the fine, oval faces, the large eyes, the short upper lip and the thin, often Apollo's bow lips, are any guide to race, they indicate a Caucasoid race."

Anthropologists are also baffled by the apparent presence of Caucasoid peoples in the prehistoric Pacific. Genetic testing conducted during the 1990s showed traces of Basque DNA in the people of Easter Island and greater Polynesia.

These age-old, oral traditions are not only being underscored by the latest strides made in genetic research, but combining to show that the prehistory of the Americas and its Caucasian and giant heritage is far richer than previously suspected.

The preponderance of Caucasian racial types and European blood in ancient America is only part of the story, however. Scientists of the North Atlantic Biocultural Organisation (NABO) have made it clear that Asiatic migration via the Bering Strait was not the only possible path taken by prehistoric peoples into the New World. If this is true, could Kennewick Man, the nine-thousand-year-old Caucasoid skeleton found on the banks of Washington State's Columbia River, be related to the oldest cultures of Western Europe? A definitive answer may be forthcoming in a new theory concerning North America's human origins that addresses the dispersal of peoples across the continent from a circumpolar culture. This theory tackles not only mass migration between Asia and North America, but also interbreeding and the establishment of hybrid cultures.

Examination of human mitochondria may prove a Caucasoid link to the first Americans, who date as far back as 28,000 BCE. Known as the "power packs" of DNA, these organelles within cells helped scientists develop four categories of ancestral groups, or lineages, for Native Americans. Congruent with existing dogma and fueling arguments in favor of Asiatic origins for the New World population, these lineages can be traced back to Siberia and Northeast Asia, specifically the Baikal and Altai-Sayan regions.

However, a fifth lineage is also recognized among the founding genetic strains of Native Americans. Known as "haplogroup X," this genetic signature is the vestige of either a later population found in Europe and the Middle East or a primeval population of Caucasoid ethnicity that inhabited Asia. Most Americans have been taught the Bering Strait theory as the sole explanation for the peopling of the continent, and are thus unaware that it is no longer entirely accepted, even by scientific dogmatists. Archaeological finds in South America and along the North American Eastern Seaboard show conclusively that there were several distinct and separate migrations of different racial groups to the Americas during prehistory.

Furthermore, recent studies point to the hypothesis of a North Atlantic Crescent, composed of water and ice, which may have served as a "bridge" that connected Europe with the Americas. In December 2000, archaic-cartographers of the National Geographic Society mapped a "European theory" for the possible migration of at least some Native American peoples. *Scientific American, Discovering Archaeology,* with its January 2, 2000, issue, had already broached the notion of an Atlantic passage. It depicted northern island-hopping routes from Iceland to Greenland, then Labrador, which are still possible today by following areas covered in ice. This theory is entirely plausible in that Arctic waters provide an abundance of seafood, enabling travelers to eat as they go, as exhibited in the Inuit migration from Alaska to Greenland some eight hundred to one thousand years ago.

This sudden turnabout—the admission of a possible alternate diffusion to the Americas—followed hard on the discovery of a "rare X-factor" in mitochondrial DNA among indigenous peoples of both Northern Europe and North America, and demonstrates a fundamental shift in mainstream scientific opinion. The "X pattern," or "European X lineage," joins the already well-known linkage of type O blood among North American natives (or type B, if from Asia) and modern aboriginal populations along the Atlantic fringe of Europe (the mountainous border of Norway and Sweden, the west coast of Ireland, and the Pyrenees Mountains). This "X pattern" link clearly proves that Europeans populated the Americas at some point in our collective past.

Referred to variously as "Old European," "modern Cro-Magnon," or "Paleo-Atlantid," the race associated with this "X pattern" is made up of tall, heavy-browed individuals, with ruddy complexions and brunette hair. Light eyes are possible but not mandatory. The percentage of Rh negative blood is high. (Rh negative blood is rare.) Transatlantic migrations involving these ancient genotypes are enumerated by a growing frequency of genetic comparisons with North American aboriginal tribes. In Newfoundland, descendants from at least one of these migrations survived until their forcible extinction in 1829. They spoke a linguistic isolate bearing no connection to nearby mainland peoples, whether Inuit (Eskimo) or Algonquian.

Genetic sequencing of haplotypes reveals that more than one migratory event took place. As one DNA study states, "The notion of a homogeneous, Amerindian genetic pool does not conform with these and other results" (Callegari-Jacques et al. 1993). Mummies of Caucasoid persons have been found at South America's pre-Columbian cities, some of which appear to have been populated by more than fifty thousand residents. These ruins continue to yield atypical evidence supporting the theory that many of America's ancient civilizations were founded by seafaring peoples with long traditions of open-water voyages. Rather than walking ten thousand miles from Mongolia to Chile, the first Americans may have sailed first class. And where they came from will soon be firmly resolved by DNA testing.

From red-headed mummies in Peru's pre-Inca graves to blond-headed Toltec warrior-priests in central Mexico, this is not the history of our parents' generation. Pre-Columbian tombs are shattering the adage that "dead men tell no tales." Great steps in understanding the real origins of America are being made. They are striding over the academically dead corpses of fearful, politically correct social historians, who now find themselves haunted by the long-dead bodies of Stone Age Americans. Some archaeologists have built their academic and financial empires on theories presently invalidated by modern genetics.

DNA research has placed all upholders of the old paradigm under siege. And when the lab results are in, they will be out looking for job retraining.

THE GIANT MOUND BUILDERS OF ERIE

Some of the most significant archaeological artifacts yet discovered in North America were found in various Pennsylvania townships during the latter half of the nineteenth century. Rev. Robin Swope, a Pittsburgh paranormal investigator, recently encountered the following article while doing research on ancient gravesites near Philadelphia & Erie Road:

> When the roadway of the Philadelphia & Erie road, where it passes through the Warfel farm, was being widened, another deposit of bones was dug up and summarily deposed of as before (Thrown in a neighboring ditch). Among the skeletons was one of a giant, side by side with a smaller one, probably that of his

wife. The arm and leg bones of this Native American Goliath were about one-half longer than those of the tallest man among the laborers; the skull was immensely large; the lower jawbone easily slipped over the face and whiskers of a full-faced man, and the teeth were in a perfect state of preservation. Another skeleton was dug up in Conneaut Township a few years ago that was quite as remarkable in its dimensions. As in the other instance, a comparison was made with the largest man in the neighborhood, and the jawbone readily covered his face, while the lower bone of the leg was nearly a foot longer than the one with which it was measured, indicating that the man must have been eight to ten feet in height.

The bones of a flathead were turned up in the same township some two years ago with a skull of unusual size. Relics of a former time have been gathered in that section by the panful, and among other curiosities a brass watch was found that was as big as a common saucer. An ancient graveyard was discovered in 1820, on the land now known as Dr. Carter and Dr. Dickinson places in Erie, which created quite a sensation at the time. Dr. Albert Thayer dug up some of the bones, and all indicated a race of beings of immense size. (History of Erie County 1884, 166–69)

DISCOVERIES IN MARION COUNTY, WEST VIRGINIA, 1852–1974

Marion County, West Virginia, was once the epicenter of an ancient civilization, as indicated by the archaeological evidence. Examples of the unique engineering skills of this early society include earthen forts, burial mounds, and macadamized roadways. Pictographs, inscribed stones, and even giant skeletons have also been discovered (Authentic Artifact Collectors Association).

This hints at the possibility of an advanced culture of giants. We find evidence of this in the 1850s, when workers excavating a root cellar in Palatine (East Fairmont) unearthed the entombed remains of two individuals who measured more than seven feet in height. The collection of bones vanished several days later, but not before an extensive examination had been performed. These relics did not display any degree of physical abnormality despite their tremendous size. Rather, the bones indicated that this was a normal racial characteristic, their morphology perhaps even indicative of a separate species entirely (Authentic Artifact Collectors Association).

These finds were backed up in 1875 when workers discovered three giant skeletons while constructing a bridge near the mouth of the Paw Paw Creek at Rivesville. Unearthed in heavy clay soil, they still had faint wisps of reddish hair clinging to their skulls. These remains survived and were determined to be more than eight feet in height (Authentic Artifact Collectors Association).

In his weekly newsletter, "People of One Fire," architect and author Richard Thornton often suggests that the Creek Indians of ancient times were eastern North America's genuine race of giants. He is a member of the Perdido Bay Muscogee-Creek Tribe. In a private memo to the author of this book he writes:

The Creeks have produced some of the tallest "normal" Homo sapiens that have walked the earth. By normal, I mean there was no hormonal imbalance. Their inherent genes programmed them to be of natural proportions, but 7 feet or more in height. This statement is based both on the discovery of seven foot tall skeletons in ancestral Creek burials such as Etowah and Ocmulgee, plus eyewitness accounts of Spanish, French and English explorers. As a whole, the Georgia Creeks averaged a foot taller than the Europeans who first came to the New World. The general of the Creek forces in the Revolution in Georgia was 93 years old and 7 feet tall. An un-natural selection occurred during the violent period of the late 1700s and early 1800s. Extremely tall men had an advantage in hand to hand combat, but were more vulnerable to musket balls. The Creek men who carried DNA programming super height were disproportionately killed in battle.

We are still much taller than the Caucasian population in the USA on average, but don't see as many 7 footers. Nevertheless, 6'6"–6'7" is not that uncommon. Creek women are not exceptionally tall, except for those who are descended from the mountain branches of the Creek Confederacy. Where did this height come from? In our tradition, we, in the past had extensive contact with extremely tall extraterrestrials from another galaxy. Some intergalactic visitors mated with the ancestors of the Creeks, giving them their height. They also taught us advanced mathematics. Creek calendars were equally accurate as those today. We had a zero, a 10 based numerical system, knowledge of trigonometry and geometry, plus two types of writing systems. One worked like the bar code system in supermarkets, but also contained colors that transmitted information. The other was more like the early systems in Iberia and Tuscany.

They originally arrived by spacecraft, but eventually built star gates on top of massive spiral mounds at Ichese (Ocmulgee National Monument) and on the Savannah River at its confluence with the Broad River, near Elberton, GA. Some Keepers (priests) of the Wind Clan were taught how to travel to the other galaxy, but it was a dangerous trip for homo sapiens. Some never returned or returned dead/horribly deformed. The symbol of the Wind Clan is a spiral galaxy surrounded by stars and smaller galaxies. There is no way that a human on earth would know that a galaxy is spiral shaped unless they were outside our galaxy (or somebody's galaxy) looking back. Supposedly, the star gates were dismantled before Europeans began to arrive in the Americas.

As we have seen, the Native American links to giants make fascinating reading. Following are a few more.

NEWSPAPER ACCOUNTS OF GIANTS FROM THE NINETEENTH CENTURY

The following account is from the *St. John Daily News,* dated September 13, 1878. Its headline: "The Indian Chief Chickasawba: Skeletons Eight and Ten Feet in Height."

Two miles west of Barfield Point, in Arkansas County, Ark, on the east bank of the lovely stream called Pemiscott River, stands an Indian mound, some twenty-five feet high and about an acre in area at the top. This mound is called Chickasawba, and from it the high and beautiful country surrounding some twelve square miles in area, derives its name, Chickasawba.

The mound derives its name from Chickasawba, a chief of the Shawnee tribe, who lived, died, and was buried there. This chief was one of the last of the race of hunters who lived in that beautiful region, and who once peopled it quite thickly, for Indians we mean.

From 1820 to 1831 he and his hunters assembled annually at Barfield Point, then as now the principle shipping place of the surrounding country, and bartered off their furs, peltries, buffalo robes and honey to the white settlers and the trading boats on the river, receiving in return powder, shot, lead, blankets, money, etc. Aunt Kitty Williams, who now resides there, relates that Chickasawba would frequently bring in for sale at one time as much as twenty gallons of pure honey in deer-skin bags slung to his back. He was always a firm friend of the whites, a man of gigantic stature and herculean strength. In his nineteenth year he took a young wife and by her had two children.

In 1831 she died, and the old chief did not long survive her, dying in the same year, aged 93 or 94 years. Mr. W. Fitzgerald, who moved in that country in 1822, says that up to the time of his death, Chickasawba supplied him with game. He was buried at the foot of the mound on which he lived, by the tribe, most of whom departed for the Nation immediately after performing the funeral rites. A few, however, lingered there up to a late date, the last of them, we believe, being John East, who, in 1860, at the breaking out of the war, joined Captain Charley Bowen's company of the late "so-called" and fought the war through, as a gallant a "reb" as any of them, coming back home in 1866 to return to the arts of peace.

Chickasawba was perfectly honest, and the best informed chief of his tribe. His contemporary chiefs were Long Knife, Sunshine, Corn Meal, Moonshine, etc. Mike Brennan and Quill buried him. He left a son named John Pemscott.

A number of years ago, in making an excavation into or near the foot of Chickasawba's mound, a portion of a gigantic human skeleton was found. The men who were digging becoming interested, unearthed the entire skeleton, and from measurements given us by reliable parties the frame of the man to whom it belonged could not have been less than eight or nine feet in height. Under the skull, which easily slipped over the head of our informant, was found a peculiarly shaped earthen jar, resembling nothing in the way of Indian pottery which had before been seen by them. It was exactly the shape of the round bodied, long necked carafes or water decanters, a specimen of which may be seen on Gatson's dining table.

The material of which the vase was made was a peculiar kind of clay, and the workmanship was very fine. The belly or body of it was ornamented with figures or hieroglyphics consisting of a correct delineation of human hands, parallel to each other, open palms outward, and running up and down the vase, the wrists to the base and the fingers towards the neck. On either side of the hands were tibiae or thigh bones, also correctly delineated, running around the base. There were other things found with the skeleton, but this is all that our informant remembers. Since that time wherever an excavation has been made in the Chickasawba country in the neighborhood of the mound similar skeletons have been found, and under the skull of every one were found similar funeral vases, almost exactly like the one described.

There are now in this city several of the vases and portions of the huge skeletons. One of the editors of the Appeal (newspaper) yesterday measured a thigh bone, which is fully three feet long. The thigh and shin bones, together with bones of the foot, stood up in a proper position in a physician's office in this city, measure five feet in height and show the body to which the leg belonged to have been nine to ten feet height.

At Beaufort's Landing, near Barfield, in digging up the leg of which measured between five and six feet in length, and other bones in proportion. In a few days we hope to be able to lay before our readers accurate measurements of skeletons now in the city and of the articles found in the graves. It is not a matter of doubt that these are human remains but of a long extinct race; a race which flourished, lived and died many centuries ago.

Here is another newspaper account from the nineteenth century. It was published in the *Huron Expositor Newspaper* in Ontario, Canada, on October 13, 1893. Its headline: "Men of Great Stature Found at Two Large Burial Sites in Nebraska."

A farmer plowing near Calhoun, Nebraska recently turned up a human skull, and search revealed a large number of other skulls, besides bones. These relics were those of a powerful race, and who they were is unknown. The skulls are large but the forehead is extremely low. A World-Herald reporter visited the place, and a measurement was taken of one of the lower jaws found and compared with the dimensions taken of one of the men on the field. The relic's jaw was found to be an inch larger each way in proportion, than that of the person whose measurement has been taken, although he was six feet three inches in height, weighed nearly 200 pounds, and had unusually large jaws. The measurement of the lower maxillary found is as follows: depth, 4 inches; width inside measure from wisdom tooth to wisdom tooth 2¼ inches; total length of jaw, 5½ inches. The upper was fully as large, while the teeth resembled those of a cow more than those of a human being. They were badly worn and would go to show that the owner ate meat, presumably buffalo, a great deal. A dentist when shown the teeth said that they were much larger than any of those of a white person living in this age.

A theory advanced is that these are the remains of some Mandan Indians, who were the earliest settlers of this part of the country, but were ultimately exterminated by the Sioux. The size of these bones would explode this theory, however, as the Mandans were not a large race [Indeed, nor were they racially aberrant in any manner with normal cranium and teeth]. Another theory is that they are perhaps, the remains of northwestern Indians who were killed by another tribe. This tribe was large in stature, according to tradition, many being six feet and more in height.

The reporter found about fifty feet from the location of this trench another in which were buried the remains of five grown persons and one infant. A spade plied to the earth soon brought to view the remains of six human beings. These skulls were smaller and not of such extraordinary thickness as those exhumed from the first trench. They also bore the appearance of having lain in the ground for a long period, as they would crumble apart of their own weight, while those first discovered were in a fair state of preservation. The cavities of the skulls had become filled with dirt, and it was only with great care in handling that a very fair specimen was preserved. The trench was three feet-square and about two feet deep. In order to place a human body into so small a grave it must have been fearfully mutilated. When found the arms were over the head, while the tibia and fibula were found under all. The skulls were also found in different positions, some being straight up and straight down, while others were lying face up and face down. No pottery, metal or the like was found by which they could be classified with the mound builders (300 BCE–500 CE).

MUMMIES OF THE AMERICAN SOUTHWEST

In 1931, an ancient repository of mummified male giants was discovered in the American Southwest. (No female remains were found.) The man credited with finding the mummies was a retired Cincinnati physician named F. Bruce Russell. The subterranean shafts that held the relics for millennia were located directly beneath the Colorado Desert. These relics were between eight and nine feet tall. Dr. Daniel S. Bovee, who participated in excavations at New Mexico's famous cliff dwellings, reportedly dated the mummies to around eighty thousand years old. They were discovered along with a number of implements that also were placed at around the eighty-thousand-year mark. Dr. Howard E. Hill said, regarding the ancient remains: "These giants are clothed in garments consisting of a medium length jacket and trousers extending slightly below the knees. The texture of the material is said to resemble gray dyed sheepskin, but obviously it was taken from an animal unknown today" (Childress 1991, 496).

Hill also claimed that another cavern was found in an elaborately constructed ritual hall, obviously utilized by the same civilization to which the gigantic mummies belonged.

Among its devices and markings were symbols not dissimilar to those used by the Freemasons, and hieroglyphs found at the site seem to indicate a melding of both Mesoamerican and Egyptian style, with some Mesopotamian influence. The hieroglyphs in question had been chiseled on carefully polished granite (Childress 1991, 496).

Hill affirmed that the explorers of the site believe this was a cemetery for the tribe's racial hierarchy. Such an elite ruling class did not include women, obviously, as again, the remains of women weren't found here. The temple wasn't the only structure found at the site. "A long tunnel from this temple took the party into a room where some catastrophe apparently drove people into the caves. All of the implements of their civilization were found" (Childress 1991, 496).

Hill proudly proclaimed that what the team had ultimately discovered might be "the fabled lost continent of Atlantis." In fact, Hill continued, "This discovery may be more important than the unveiling of King Tut's tomb" (Childress 1991, 497). Such bombastic claims did not go over well with the archaeological establishment, of course, which has such a grip on our mainstream media. It is now hoped that the Internet may help to alleviate this deficit between the controlled media and free thought.

MORE GIANTS' BONES UNEARTHED IN THE AMERICAN WEST

In 1898 the brothers H. Flagler Cowden and Charles C. Cowden undertook one of the most profoundly interesting series of excavations in North American history. This sibling team of scientists, studying the antiquity of desert populations, conducted archaeological excavations in the desolate and barren Death Valley and allegedly uncovered the skeletal remains of a giant woman, 7.5 feet tall. The Cowdens theorized that she was a member of "the race of unprecedented large primitives which vanished from the face of the earth some 100,000 years ago" (Childress 1991, 500).

The amount of silica in the soil and sands, the state of petrifaction of the skeleton, and the crystallization and opalization of the bone marrow helped the two scientists determine the age of the woman's remains, which were found at a depth of five feet in a "hard-rock formation of conglomerate containing small amounts of silica, which required a longer time to petrify than normal desert sands" (Childress 1991, 500).

In *Lost Cities and Ancient Mysteries of the Southwest*, Childress quotes author Brad Steiger: "Ed Earl Repp, a writer, told of the 'honor and privilege' that were his in working with the Cowden brothers; in the June 1970 issue of *Wild West* magazine he recalled that 'in the same earth-strata where the giant female skeleton was found, they also recovered the remains of prehistoric camels and mammals of . . . an elephant-like creature with four tusks. . . . With them were the remains of petrified palm trees, towering ferns, and prehistoric fishlike creatures.'"

The Cowdens theorized that in times of vast antiquity when the lost race of giants lived there, Death Valley may have been an inlet of the Pacific Ocean, for in the same area in which they found the skeleton of the giant females they also unearthed the petrified remains of marine life.

The two brothers also found that the giant woman's skeleton bore a number of anomalous physical appendages and attributes not found in contemporary humans. She had several extra "buttons" at the base of her spine, and her canine teeth were twice the length of those of modern humans.

The Cowdens hypothesized that when the California we know today was formed—as the mountains rose and the sea retreated—what had been the tropical climate left the region. The steaming swamps were replaced by wastelands, which still remain in much of the southern portion of the state (Childress 1991, 500–501).

Another account of an ancient giant unearthed in California is as follows: In July 1895, a team of miners excavated the entombed skeletal remains of a woman who stood six feet eight inches tall. The discovery took place in a mine not far from the town of Bridlevale Falls, California.

In his book *Montezuma's Serpent and Other True Supernatural Tales of the Southwest,* Brad Steiger reports:

G. E. Martindale, who was in charge of the miners, noticed a pile of stones that seemed to have been placed against the wall of a cliff in an unnatural formation. Assuming that the rock had been stacked by human hands, Martindale ordered his men to begin removing the stones in order to investigate what might lie beyond the formation.

The miners were astonished when they found a wall of rock that had been shaped and fitted together with apparent knowledge of fine masonry technique. Convinced that they had stumbled upon some lost treasure trove, they set about tearing down the wall so that they might claim their riches. Instead of ingots of gold or trunks of jewels, the men found a mummified corpse of a very large woman lying on a ledge that had been carved from natural stone. The corpse had been wrapped in animal skins and covered with a very fine powder. She was clutching a child to her breast. When the mummy was taken to Los Angeles, scientists agreed that the woman was a member of a giant race that had thrived on this continent long before the American Indian had become the dominant inhabitant. They concluded that the mummy's height of six feet eight inches would have represented a height in life of at least seven feet. Figuring the classic height difference between men and women, they supposed that the males of the forgotten species would been nearly eight feet tall. (Childress 1991, 501–2)

In the 1950s, a popular anti-Darwinist and creationist author, Clifford Burdick, contended that amateur archaeologists had collected substantial physical evidence proving the existence of a race of giants in antiquity. These consisted of a number of now extinct races of giants he identifies with the Greek Titans, the frost and mountain giants of ancient Germanic lore, "who cut a swath through Jotunheim," as well as the ancient Chinese race that was "twice as tall as us" (Time-Life 1991, 25).

Burdick investigated the work of several hobbyists who claimed to have plaster casts of gigantic footprints, some supposedly found beside dinosaur tracks. Between 1938 and 1950, a Texan by the name of Jim Ryals found several such tracks in sediments along the banks of the Paluxy River southwest of Dallas. The footprints were some sixteen inches long and eight inches wide. Alongside them were the prints of a three-toed dinosaur or other primordial reptile.

Examples of gigantic footprints and similar archaeological finds are abundant throughout the Western deserts, yet few mainstream paleontologists accept them as genuine. They insist they are fakes, especially when faced with the assertion that they were found alongside dinosaurs, which would make the footprints older than sixty-five million years, hinting at the supposed impossibility that humans and dinosaurs were contemporaneous.

In this chapter we have discussed many accounts of giants in North America. They would indicate to even the most casual observer that we were in fact preceded by a race of historical giants. There can be little doubt of the validity of these claims, nor their importance to the heritage of our nation and the world. But it is tricky business, being a proponent of the idea that giants once roamed the Earth, in a world in which the firmly entrenched establishment takes no quarter, no prisoners, in their attempt to intellectually subjugate the masses. This author believes that it is only a matter of time until the truth must and will be realized.

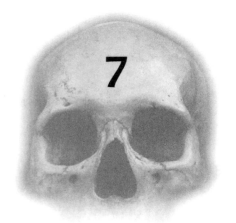

GIANTS IN OLD CENTRAL AMERICA, OLD SOUTH AMERICA, AND ANCIENT POLYNESIA

The first great waters came. They engulfed the seven islands (Atlantis). . . .
And the unholy (necromancers and militarists) were annihilated, and with them most of the huge animals born of the sweat of the Earth.

No. 46 *Stanza of Archaic and Secret Records of Old Asia*

As his strength
Failed him at length,
He met a pilgrim shadow—
"Shadow," said he,
"Where can it be—
This land of El Dorado?"

"Over the Mountains
Of the Moon,
Down the Valley of the Shadow,
Ride, boldly ride,"
The shade replied—
"If you seek for El Dorado."

EDGAR ALLAN POE, *EL DORADO*

AZTEC CREATION AND THE GIANTS

Fernando de Alva Cortés Ixtlilxóchitl, the sixteenth-century Mexican chronicler and historian and great-great-grandson of Cuitláhuac (the former Aztec ruler of Tenochtitlan), provided European scholars with varied accounts of Aztec and Central American beliefs and legends, including those of giants.

The Spanish viceroy of New Spain commissioned Ixtlilxóchitl to write a history of the indigenous people of Central America and write he did. As Ixtlilxóchitl explains, according to Aztec cosmology, creation is not a single event but rather a continual process of birth, death, and rebirth. Following the destruction of each world, the Earth is reborn by the sanctified blood sacrifice of a god, a reality mimicked by the ceremonial blood sacrifices performed by the Aztec priests. Through each death a new sun could be born, and hence a new age would begin.

According to Aztec myth, during the first age, or Sun, the gods Quetzalcoatl and Tezcatlipoca created a race of giants from ashes, giving them acorns for nourishment. But the giants so enraged the gods due to their wickedness that the gods decided to end the giants' existence and sent the jaguars to destroy them. Only seven survived the onslaught of the savage beasts. Later, when the gods summoned forth the waters to flood the Earth and destroy the first race of humans, these seven giants, the Xelhua, climbed the mountains to seek refuge from the thrashing waters that were enveloping the planet. Five of the giants survived the torrent, and in the end they built the great tower of Cholula to commemorate their survival of the flood.

Boston University geologist Robert M. Schoch discusses this myth in his book *Voyages of the Pyramid Builders* (2004). He notes that in a variation of the same myth, the race of giants built the Great Pyramid of Cholula not merely to mark their survival but also, like the Mesopotamian Tower of Babel, to reach the clouds. The mythological backdrop for the real giants of antiquity has given us great insight into the true nature of those long-forgotten times. Simply put, every myth bears some nugget of truth. Mythology is a kind of cultural GPS device that guides us through the hidden history of the human race. But mythology alone cannot give us a clear indication of where the giants came from and ultimately where they went—that great task is left up to science and what it teaches about the evolution of Earth and of humankind.

GIANTS OF CENTRAL AND SOUTH AMERICA

According to Stephen Quayle in his book *Giants: Master Builders of Prehistoric and Ancient Civilizations,* Diego Durán, a friar and early Spanish settler in the New World who grew up closely with the native population, was familiar with giant Indian tribes. He writes: "It cannot be denied that there have been giants in this country. I can confirm this as an eyewitness, for I have met men of monstrous stature here. I believe that there are many in Mexico who will remember, as I do, a giant Indian who appeared in a procession of the feast of Corpus Christi. He appeared dressed in yellow silk and a halberd at his shoulder and a helmet on his head. And he was all of three feet taller than the others" (Quayle 2002, 288).

Durán lived more closely with the native population than perhaps any of his contemporaries, and his accounts of the indigenous beliefs of the Aztecs and other Central American groups are by far the most well-respected among modern historians. Many who lived at the same time, Bernardino de Sahagún and José de Acosta among them, recalled vividly the days when Central America was dominated by a cult-driven center of giants who predominated over Aztec and earlier Toltec and Olmec civilizations.

According to the Aztecs, originally giants and a bestial people of average size dominated the region. Then in 902 CE, emigrants from Teocolhuacan, also known as Aztlán, or in European terms, the lost civilization of Atlantis—which is "found toward the north and near the region of La Florida (where Edgar Cayce proposed it would be found)"—began to arrive in Mexico. According to Quayle, these six kindred tribes included the Xochimilca, the Chalca, the Tepanec, the Colhua, the Tlahuica, and the Tlaxcalans. A seventh tribe, the Aztecs, were brothers to these people, but they "came to live here three hundred and one years after the arrival of the others" (Quayle 2002, 289).

According to Durán: "They recorded to their painted books the type of land and kind of people they found there." These books show two types of people, one from the west of the snow-covered mountains toward Mexico, and the other from the east, where Puebla and Cholula are found. Those from the first were the Chichimecs, and people from Puebla and Cholula were the giants, or *Quiname,* which means "men of great stature."

In support of this, in his 1952 book, *Secret Cities of Old South America,* Harold T. Wilkins writes:

In the fall of 1929, Dean Byron Cummings of Arizona University and Professor Manuel San Domingo, a Mexican Government scientist of Sonora, went to a dangerous spot 160 miles from the international border where the turbulent Yaquis smash excavation work with rifle butts and menace intruders with sudden death. They found three giant skeletons of two men and one woman eight feet tall. The skulls were a foot long and ten inches wide, and three were remains of six children, all six feet tall. In tall ollas were human ashes suggesting either cremation or human sacrifices. The remains were in an ancient burial ground called "Cyclopes necropolis." Beautiful ceramics were buried with the giants' remains which were also covered with fine jewels.

Earlier in the same year (1929) Mr. Paxon Hayes found mummies of a peculiar race of Mongoloid giants in dry caves in the sierras of New Mexico, USA. He got out 34 of these mummies, and did four years' hard work in the region. He saw facial angles of these and their burial customs are different from those of the Indians. They have slanting eyes and sloping foreheads, and the adults are about seven feet high, though their feet are only seven inches long. Their hair is black, with a peculiarly sun-burnt tinge when closely examined. The remains were preserved in asphalt, or resin, and wrapped in burial cloths bound with fiber. (Childress 2010)

Wilkins also notes, "Telegrams from Casas Grandes, Mexico, in 1923, announced the discovery of several skeletons of *Indians fifteen feet tall,* buried side by side, with vases of precious stones. The news came from Ciudad Juarez" (Childress 2010).

GIANTS OF PATAGONIA

Perhaps the most intriguing mystery involving a lost race of giants in South America involves those of Patagonia, an area of southern Argentina and Chile where European explorers repeatedly reported encountering native Indians of tremendous stature. The very name Patagonia points to the persistent rumors of giants in the region, for Patagonia means "Land of the People with Long Feet" (Childress 2010).

Ferdinand Magellan discovered Patagonia in 1520, during his monumental journey around the Earth. While his fleet lay at anchor in the natural harbor, he witnessed a startling sight: a native, gigantic in stature, approached him. Figafetta, a companion of Magellan, reported that "This man was so tall that our heads scarcely came up to his waist, and his voice was like that of a bull." Later, Magellan learned from normal-sized natives that the giant belonged to a neighboring tribe. "Remarkably," science writer Terrence Aym writes, "Magellan's logs show that he and his crew captured two of these living giants and brought them aboard ship, intending to bring them back to Europe. Unfortunately, the giants grew ill and they both died during the return voyage. Magellan had their remains buried at sea" (Childress 2010).

The later British explorer Sir Francis Drake anchored in the same harbor as Magellan had several decades earlier. In 1578, in that same vicinity, Drake reported seeing natives of unusually high stature, some seven feet tall or more. Another individual, Anthony Knyvel, who participated in an exploratory mission to the Strait of Magellan in 1592, claimed to have witnessed, firsthand, Patagonians from ten to twelve feet in height. He was also said to have measured bodies of the same size at Port Desire, in modern-day Argentina. Additional skeletons, ten or eleven feet long, were discovered in 1615 by two crewmen from the Dutch schooner Wilhelm Schouten (Childress 2010).

It is clear from these reports that the remnants of an ancient race of giants were well established during this period. However, for nearly 150 years after this last sighting, no further reports were made of the Patagonian giants. Other natives of Patagonia were of normal size, but even they regularly maintained that a race of primordial giants inhabited the interior of the land (Childress 2010).

TIAHUANACO: LAND OF THE GIANTS

One place on Earth raises the bar on the question of whether giants once inhabited the world. It is the ancient fallen city of Tiahuanaco, which is a few short miles from the shores of Lake Titicaca in the

Andean highlands of Bolivia, not far from the Ecuadorian border.

From the early reports we have of the city, wherein it is described with obvious amazement, we learn that it was popularly understood to have been the dwelling place of giants. The first recorded account that comes down to us was written by the Spanish chronicler Pedro Cieza de León, who visited it in 1549:

> Tiahuanaco is not a small village, rather it is famous for its grandiose buildings. . . . A short distance from a hill stand two stone statues shaped as men. . . . They are so large they look like giants. . . . But the thing that elicits the greatest amount of wonder is the size [of the stone slabs], which are so huge we cannot understand how men could ever have moved them. Many of these platforms have been worked in various ways. . . . There are also stone slabs with doorways, all made from a single block. . . . We do not comprehend with which tools such work could have been achieved. . . . What's more, the blocks must have been even greater in size before they were worked. . . . No one understands how these great weights could ever have been moved. . . .
>
> I have been assured that these constructions were already there before the Inca ruled, and much of what the Inca later erected in Cuzco had been inspired by what they had seen in Tiahuanaco. . . . In the presence of Juan Varagas, I asked the natives whether these buildings had been erected during the age of the Incas: they laughed and answered, the buildings had been there for many years before the Incas began their rule. These structures, they assured me, and they knew this with certainty from their forefathers, had been built in a single night, constructed by beings whose provenance they did not know. And may the fame of these things remain intact throughout the universe. . . . There were none still living who knew this unearthly site as anything other than ruins." (Däniken 2010, 42–43)

In book 1, chapter 23, of his work on the subject, historian Garcilaso de la Vega (El Inca) wrote of Tiahuanaco:

I looked in wonder at a great wall built of such mighty stones that we could not imagine which earthly power could have been used to accomplish such a feat. . . . The natives maintain that the buildings were there before the Incas. . . . They do not know who the builders were, but know with some degree of certainty from their ancestors that all these wonders were erected in a single night. (de la Vega 1723)

It is easy to interpret the undertones. These chroniclers were confident that some greater forces, or group of forces, were at hand here. . . . It seems likely that they were.

Another account of Tiahuanaco comes from author Harold T. Wilkins. In his book *Mysteries of Ancient South America* (1947, 187), he describes an encounter at Tiahuanaco with a "colossal statue, wearing a strangely inflated skullcap, one hand clasping to his breast a scepter of a condor-head, the other a tablet with hieroglyphics." This colossus, according to native sources, represents a giant master race that was known as the *Ra-mac*. This is similar to the name of the sun god *Ra-Mu* that, according to the Sanskrit writings of India, was the chief deity of the drowned Pacific continent of Mu, or Lemuria. *Ra,* of course, was the sun god of ancient Egypt and the earlier Osirian Empire. In addition to depictions of gigantic proportions, statuettes of black men were also found in Tiahuanaco—"the cradle of mankind"—which may also be of Lemurian origin (Wilkins 1952, 110).

ARCHAEOLOGICAL EXCAVATIONS AT TIAHUANACO, 1904–1945

Two individuals are credited with offering some of the most extreme views concerning the antiquity and origin of Tiahuanaco, although they most certainly were not the only ones to do so. Engineer and avocational archaeologist Arthur Posnansky and German archaeologist Dr. Edmund Kiss were considered to be the dominant and unconventional authorities of Tiahuanaco prehistory in the early to mid-1900s. These two men of uncompromising resolve single-handedly rewrote the books on Tiahuanaco. Posnansky was the Royal Bavarian Professor of geodesic engineering from 1904 to 1945 and a man of many interests. For him, Tiahuanaco was much more than a collection of fabulous ruins that had possibly been erected by giants. It was, as he called it, "the cradle of humanity."

"Tiahuanaco," Posnansky affirmed, "is the greatest sun temple ever to be constructed by mankind—not just in South America, but in the whole world" (Däniken 2010, 55). He went on to report that the native population had named their temple "Akapana," which in the ancient Aymara language means "the place where the observers dwell."

Dr. Edmund Kiss spent nine years studying in the Andes and excavating at the site of Tiahuanaco. Part of his research involved the monolithic gateway known as "the Gateway of the Sun." Kiss believed that the inscriptions and symbols on the sun gate were features of a complex calendar, though initially he was unsure what type of calendar it might be. At one point, Kiss concluded that it was in fact an ice age calendar predicting the cycles of the sun, moon, and stars—and as such it marked the coming of the winter and summer solstices.

This provided the scientific basis of yet another theory. Kiss calculated that Tiahuanaco was built in 27,000 BCE and believed that the city had been overswept by a great flood early in its history, approximately eighteen thousand years in the past. Although Posnansky only partially agreed with this view, further research confirmed this dating. Evidence suggested that the city's dominant feature was a sun temple: the great Kalasasaya—a name inspired by a connection to the inundated continent of Mu. This temple comprises the vast stadium of present-day

Tiahuanaco, which was constructed between 21,600 BCE and 2800 BCE—a range of 18,800 years (Wilkins 1947, 18).

Colonel Percy Fawcett, an adventurer and amateur archaeologist of the early twentieth century, goes even further: "These megalithic ruins of Tiahuanaco," says Fawcett, "were never built on the Andes at all. They are part of a great city submerged ages ago in the Pacific Ocean. When the crust of the earth up heaved and created the great Andean cordilleras, these ruins were elevated from the bed of the ocean to where you see them" (Wilkins 1947, 186). If Fawcett is indeed correct, then the earliest stages of Tiahuanaco could date back as far as one hundred thousand years or more. As such, Tiahuanaco is the perfect laboratory for those wishing to investigate more fully the race of giants hypothesis.

THE GIANTS OF ANCIENT POLYNESIA

Having explored the Americas for traces of ancient giants, we will now turn our attention to Polynesia, comprising more than one thousand islands in the Pacific Ocean. Here we will continue to explore various historical references to giants, as well as spend some fair amount of time on one of the most enigmatic archaeological anomalies on the planet: the very large human figures made of stone on Easter Island, called the *Moai*.

EASTER ISLAND: HOME TO ARCHAIC CAUCASOIDS

Some 4,000 kilometers southeast of Nan Madol, with its canals and temples constructed of basalt logs, and 3,782 kilometers from the wind-swept coast of Chile lies the enigma known as Easter Island, a place that has fascinated and perplexed visitors for more than two centuries. It is also one of the most geographically remote and culturally isolated places on Earth. This island's native inhabitants are of Polynesian ancestry, but centuries of isolation have allowed them to evolve separately into their own distinct race. Although there is evidence of contact between the islanders and foreign visitors, and varying types of ethnicity are exhibited within the native population, including Caucasian traits, their culture remains distinct.

The gigantic Moai, or stone statues of Easter Island, have origins that stretch far back into human antiquity. These cyclopean statues seem to hint at some unspeakable connection with a vanished race of giants. The magnificent and colossal stone figures are 11 to 22 meters high and weigh as much as 45 tons. Despite repeated speculation by mainstream scientists, the reality is that no one knows for certain who built them, how, or why. Furthermore, how ancient is the occupation of the island, and who were its earliest inhabitants?

Today, this tiny speck of land in the middle of the South Pacific known as Easter Island is also called Rapa Nui in the native tongue, meaning "Land of the Bird Men."

The official records attribute the island's discovery to the Dutch vessel *Afrikaansche Galei,* under the command of Admiral Jacob Roggeveen. The discovery occurred on Easter Day, April 5, 1722, at 5:00 p.m. In commemoration of its day of discovery, Roggeveen dubbed this tiny speck of land Easter Island. The following day, after visiting the island, he attempted to describe its material culture:

> Concerning the religion of these people, of this we could get no full knowledge because of the shortness of our stay, we merely observed that they set fires before some particularly high erected stone images. . . . These stone images at first caused us to be struck with astonishment, because we could not comprehend how it was possible that these people, who are devoid of heavy thick timber for making any machines, as well as strong ropes, nevertheless had been able to erect such images, which were fully thirty feet high and thick in proportion. (Flenley and Bahn 2003)

After coming ashore, the Dutch sailors, together with their officers, spent a considerable amount of time touring the twenty-five mile island, marveling at its monuments and writing down firsthand accounts of the gigantic figures and the peculiar writings used by the natives. They also had the opportunity to have sexual intercourse with a number of the native females, as tribute from the chieftains and the gods. The Dutch explorers reported that the islanders wore very little clothing and inhabited reed huts (Flenley and Bahn 2003). Tragically, the first contact with these indigenous peoples ended in gunfire and the killing of about one hundred or so Rapa Nui islanders. David Hatcher Childress explains that Roggeveen ordered his sailors to fire into a crowd of natives who were engaged in thievery and touching and toying with the ship and its technology, mainly out of curiosity (Childress 1988, 118).

One of the most obvious realities of the people present on the island was their mixed racial heritage. A large number of the native people appeared Caucasian, while others, fewer in number, had brown or red skin. There were many intermediary groups. A long-eared group was tall and fair-skinned with ruddy cheeks. They often had brown, red, or blond hair (Joseph 2006, 170). This is but one of many out-of-place Caucasian groups that Western European explorers would encounter as they ventured to the remote corners of the Earth.

Some scholars, such as Robert Langdon, claim that Roggeveen and his ship of Dutch explorers were not the first Europeans to set foot on the island. Langdon believes that sailors from a lost Spanish caravel, the *San Lesmes,* which disappeared in 1526 and apparently ran aground in Tahiti, survived and intermarried with the Polynesian women. Langdon suggests that somehow these offspring made it to Easter Island and entered the gene pool, leaving behind traces of Basque genetic markers. This would seem incredibly complex and fanciful if not for the fact that Easter Islander DNA contains a genetic structure common within the Basque population of Western Europe (Flenley and Bahn 2003).

According to the French explorer Jean François de Galaup, comte de Lapérouse, during his visit in 1786, both the statues and people possessed a distinct European quality, which was unmistakable. Other visits were less constructive. For example, the Spanish expedition launched from Peru early in 1770 came back without any commentary or report whatsoever, and only managed to print a ship's log more than a century later, in 1908 (Flenley and Bahn 2003).

In 1774, the era of exploration and scientific investigation began in earnest. This date marked the visitation of Captain James Cook to Easter Island. He was considered the Great White God by the Pacific Islanders, as were Pizarro and Cortés by the American peoples.

On June 13, 1772, Cook departed Plymouth, England, with two ships, the *Resolution* and the *Adventure*. It was Cook's intention to sail around the world, navigate the southernmost waters, cross the Antarctic Circle, and confirm the existence of the legendary southern continent of Antarctica. They reached Easter Island on March 1, 1774. The British remained on Easter Island for only four days, as they rested and replenished what supplies they could amid the barren landscape. In his log, Cook recorded: "We could hardly conceive how these islanders, wholly unacquainted with any mechanical power, could raise such stupendous figures, and afterwards place the large cylindrical stones upon their heads" (Joseph 2006, 54).

Clearly, the bizarre nature of the island and its inhabitants baffled its European visitors. Katherine Routledge, an early twentieth-century investigator of Easter Island, put it like this: "In Easter Island, the past is the present. It is impossible to escape from it. The inhabitants of today are less real than the men who have gone. The shadows of the departed builders still possess the land" (Joseph 2006, 54). Erich von Däniken called the magnificent and colossal stone figures "robots which seem to be waiting solely to be set in motion again" (Däniken 1970, 111). Originally, the statues also wore hats, and they traditionally faced inland and not out toward the ever-crashing waves.

Dr. Jared Diamond, author of the national bestseller *Guns, Germs, and Steel,* offers up these insights into Polynesian architecture:

> The largest products of Polynesia were the immense stone struc-
> tures of a few islands—the famous giant statues of Easter Island, the
> tombs of Tongan chiefs, the ceremonial platforms of the Marque-
> sas, and the temple of Hawaii and the Societies. This monumental
> Polynesian architecture was obviously evolving in the same direction
> as the pyramids of Egypt, Mesopotamia, Mexico and Peru. Natu-
> rally, Polynesia's structures are not on the scale of those pyramids,
> but that merely reflects the fact that Egyptian pharaohs could draw
> conscript labor from a much larger human population than could
> the chief of any Polynesian island. Even so, the Easter Islanders man-
> aged to erect 24-ton stone statues—no mean feat for an island with
> only seven thousand people, who had no power source other than
> their own muscles. (Diamond 1999)

Diamond was not privy to the more alternative explanations of the monuments' origins, but his general conclusions from a mainstream standpoint are basically correct. It is also clear that had these societies been left to develop on their own, untouched by outside influence, they would have undoubtedly continued to evolve along the lines of the Mayas, Aztecs, and Old World cultures such as the Egyptians and Mesopotamians.

In *The Polynesians: Prehistory of an Island People,* Peter Bellwood says, "Easter Island society of the eighteenth century was not described as highly stratified, and was dominated by independent warring tribes who probably spent much of their time fighting over scarce resources" (1978, 113).

Bellwood divided Easter Island prehistory into three main periods. During the Early Period, 400–1100 CE, the earliest of the stone platforms were erected, and during the Middle Period, 1100–1680

CE, these platforms were equipped with the gigantic stone statues that define the island and their inhabitants to this day. During the Late Period, 1680–1868 CE, there was a drastic and devastating decline in the island's environment and the health and stability of its population, prompting the discontinuation of the peoples' religion and their traditions. The period concluded with the arrival and domination of Christian missionaries, who further undermined the native beliefs and traditions (Bellwood 1978, 114–15). This spelled certain doom for the age of giants on Easter Island.

Giants, it would seem, have been all over the globe. If they can have reached the far-flung islands of Polynesia, one might think that they must, indeed, have been anywhere, and quite possibly, everywhere. Now leaving Polynesia behind, in our next chapter we will again peer back into the mists of time to ascertain what the world might have been like before the Great Flood, and whether giants were part of this ancient landscape. Integral to this will be an assessment of those enigmatic figures known as the Watchers, and what role they may have played in humankind's earliest days. Who were they and where did they come from? Our discussion will aim to find out.

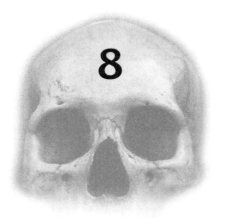

THE RACE OF
ANTEDILUVIAN GIANTS

Theirs was the giant race, before the flood.

JOHN DRYDEN, *EPISTLE TO CONGREVE*

THE WORLD BEFORE ADAM AND EVE

In the Bible, we catch glimpses of an initial "First Creation" or "pre-Adamic" world that preceded the emergence of Adam. Angels and the sons of God ruled this world. According to certain biblical passages, this primordial Earth was a thriving community with vast cities and complex life-forms (Quayle 2002, 51). The following passage from the Book of Jeremiah 4:23–26 briefly demonstrates what this world could have been like:

> I beheld the earth, and, lo, it was without form and void; and the heavens, and they had no light. I beheld the mountains, and lo, they trembled, and all the hills moved lightly. I beheld, and, lo,

143

there was no man, and all the birds of the heavens were fled. I
beheld, and, lo, the fruitful place was a wilderness, and all the cities were broken down at the presence of the Lord, and by his fierce
anger.

The key phrase "I beheld, and, lo, there was no man" indicates
that Jeremiah was referring to a time that predated the emergence
of mankind. This was a near-forgotten epoch in which an entirely
different population inhabited and ruled the earth. Author Stephen
Quayle remarks that the prophet made reference to a world "without form and void." This phrase is taken directly from Genesis 1.
It therefore indicates, in Quayle's mind, that Jeremiah was referring
to a time before Adam arose from the choking dust of the Earth.
Such terminology offers a brief glimpse of that alternative world history that overturns the accepted paradigm and forces us to reexamine
long-held beliefs.

In this chapter we return to the original sources of human history
that modern science has abandoned but that nonetheless bridge the gaps
left by often dilatory twenty-first-century historians and archaeologists.
Calling upon disparate accounts, we aim to get a clearer view of what
antediluvian culture was like the world over and to determine whether
there are similar threads in these cultures that can be woven together
to posit a consistent, universal story. Part and parcel of this will be to
put the strange race known as the Watchers under close scrutiny. In this
we will also explore possible links between the Watchers of old and the
Nephilim, before launching into a discussion of the anticanonical Book
of Enoch and the Book of Giants, which was derived from a fragment
of text discovered at Qumran, among the Dead Sea Scrolls. Last we will
attempt to identify the true identity of Noah. Was he, in all truth, actually a giant?

THE ANTEDILUVIAN WORLD
IN ANCIENT GREEK ACCOUNTS

Through a study of ancient works and their accounts of the antediluvian monarchs that were integral to their culture, it is possible to glean what the world may have looked like before the Great Flood. Dardanus, as the son of the founder of the city of Dardania, in the Balkans, is a good example of one of these monarchs.

Plato explains that when the Flood engulfed the whole world, the survivors who were living on mountains, now islands, split into two groups. One accepted Dardanus's son Deimas as king of Dardania, and the other group settled on the island of Samothrace. After the floodwaters subsided, Dardanus participated in the renewal of human society. He wrote in the ancient records that the Earth was once partly ruled by the giants. To the distant ancestors of the Greeks, who came from a lost civilization along the Black Sea, the word "giant" meant a dark and unfathomable being that dated back to the primordial origins of the human race.

However, the Greek culture also included rulers of the undersea kingdom who came forth to impart wisdom and knowledge. The antediluvian lord Cecrops I founded Athens, but was said to have the upper body of a man and the lower half of a fish. He taught the Athenians writing, architecture, science, and law. He also was said to have defied Zeus and had the Greeks offer up sacrifices to him instead.

In addition to these figures in the early Greek accounts were other creatures of great antiquity who would also play a pivotal role in the antediluvian world and the preparation for human conquest of Earth. One of them was Oannes.

OANNES AND THE *BABYLONIACA*

In 350 BCE, while Alexander the Great was still on the throne of Babylon, a priest and historian of the Babylonian god Marduk was busy compiling what would become the essential historical reference book of his day: the *Babyloniaca*. This priest was Berossus and his epic work consisted of three volumes. Each was written in Greek, which was the common language of the time. The *Babyloniaca* is important for many reasons, not the least of which is that it gives us a context for the Great Flood by setting it within a time line that begins with the emergence of human kingship. According to the *Babyloniaca*, which reflects Mesopotamian belief, 432,000 years elapsed between the crowning of the first earthly king, Aloros I, and the onset of the Great Flood.*

An important figure of the *Babyloniaca* is Oannes.† It was he who, according to Babylonian mythology, gave the "Tablets of Civilization" to early humans, thereby providing them with written language, after emerging from his kingdom beneath the Persian Gulf. Oannes was a strange man and fish hybrid, and was also the leader of a group of similar creatures, "a brotherhood of semi-divine beings described as half-men, half-fish, who had been sent by the gods to teach the art of civilization to humankind before the flood. The collective name by which these creatures were known was the 'Seven Sages' and the name of their leader was Oannes" (Hancock 2002). According to the *Babyloniaca*, the Seven Sages were instrumental in the early development of the Sumern civilization.

Berossus describes the encounter with Oannes as follows:

> In the first year there appeared, from that part of the Erythaean
> Sea [today's Persian Gulf], which borders upon Babylonia, an ani-

---

*This is more than one hundred times longer than the chronology given in the Old Testament, but matches the dates found in the Book of Enoch, which we will be discussing shortly.

†The same Oannes is also present in Mayan cosmology. According to Mesoamerican tradition, Oa-ana, a name that means "He Who Has His Residence in Water," sparked Mayan civilization after surfacing from a submerged society and sharing his superb wisdom with the ancient Mesoamericans. Stories of this visitor later became confused or combined with legends of the Great White God known as Quetzalcoatl by the Aztecs, Kukulcan by the Mayas, and Viracocha by the Incas.

mal endowed with reason, by the name of Oannes. . . . Its voice was articulate and human, and an image of him has been preserved to this day. This creature spent its days among men, but ate no food, and gave them insights into letters and sciences, and arts of every kind. He taught them to build cities and temples, how to draw up laws and measure the land. He showed them how to sow the seeds and how to collect the fruits; he instructed them in everything that could humanize their lives. From that time, nothing material has been added by way of improvement to his instructions. Oannes also wrote a book about the genesis of man and the origin of civil states, which he then gave to mankind. (Däniken 2009)

Some sources indicate that Oannes and the Seven Sages did much more than impart sacred technological knowledge to the human race. They also established the five antediluvian cities described in the original Sumern text depicting the Flood and the Sumern version of the Noah story. Indeed, this hints that the engineering giants, the Nephilim, and these half-fish, half-human biological entities were closely related and possibly worked together educating and preparing the first race.

Erich von Däniken equates Oannes with an extraterrestrial visitor. This author would rather keep his origins closer to the Earth. It's possible that he represents an intelligent race* that, like the giants, is all but extinct. It is also possible, even more than likely, that Oannes is one of the legendary Watchers of biblical fame, the sons of God who mated with mortal women and produced the Nephilim, a race of giants.

---

*Other examples of this race are described in ancient sacred texts. In the holy books of the Parsees, the Avesta, a mysterious being known as Yma erupts from the waters of the sea to instruct the rulers of Earth. And according to Phoenician legend, a creature of the same origins, possessing the same innate abilities and known as Taut, also taught the kings and lords of Earth. In a third example, during the reign of Chinese emperor Fuk-hi (circa 2953 BCE), a creature called Meng-ho arose from the water, "a monster with the body of a horse and the head of a dragon, whose back was laden with tablets filled with letters" (Däniken 2009).

WHO WERE THE WATCHERS—REALLY?

In his essay "When the Sons of God Cavorted with the Daughters of Men," well-known biblical scholar Ronald S. Hendel poses the following question: "If someone asked you to name the origin of a story about gods who take human wives and then give birth to a race of semidivine heroes, you might answer: It's a Greek myth, or perhaps a Norse legend, or maybe a folktale from Africa or India. Surely this story couldn't come from the sacred scriptures of Judaism and Christianity. Or could it?" (1987)

To answer this question he offers up the following passage, Genesis 6:1–4. Here it is in full:

> When mankind began to multiply on the face of the earth, and daughters were born to them, the Sons of God saw that the daughters of men were beautiful, and they took wives of them, from any whom they chose. And Yahweh said, "My spirit will not be strong in man forever, for indeed he is but flesh. His lifetime will be 120 years. Giants were on the earth in those days, and also afterwards, when the Sons of God mated with the daughters of men and they bore children for them: these were the heroes of old, the men of renown.

According to Hendel, "For thousands of years this story has scandalized readers of the Bible and for good reason. The story appears to go against the grain of our traditional understanding of biblical religion." As Hendel attests, this story remains one of most enduring controversies of modern biblical scholarship. The term *giants* is actually a mistranslation of the Hebrew word *Nephilim,* which is derived from the Hebrew verb *nafol,* meaning "to fall." Thus, the Nephilim are often conceived of as a fallen race of giants who ruled the world prior to the Great Flood, the global deluge that engulfed the antediluvian world and finally ended their reign. However, others claim that the Nephilim were actually Greys (aliens), while still others contend that the mysterious figures were the Neanderthals of Ice Age Europe and the Near East.

The descendants of the Nephilim are known as the Emin, who are described in the King James Bible as "a people greater, and many, and tall." These descendants were also the inheritors of the antediluvian religious practices and rites that were enacted atop Seir, the sacred mountain (Joseph 2005).

While we may know who the descendants of the Nephilim were, there is some controversy as to who exactly their *ancestors* were. The Bible tells us they were a hybrid race, born of the sons of God and the daughters of men. This does not explain, however, who were the sons of God, sometimes called the Watchers. This author believes they were a superior race that inhabited the Earth since its creation and were seen as gods by our earliest ancestors.

It might even be suggested that the Watchers, rather than being any form of off-world intelligence, were a previously evolved race that originated and lived on Earth prior to the emergence of modern humans and had always been our benefactor. Perhaps tales of these gods are not stories of misinterpreted extraterrestrial visitors, but rather accounts of a now-extinct race whose individuals were at one time so utterly powerful that they were in essence gods.

In the Book of Enoch we read that the Watchers, also known as the sons of God, mated with mortal women, and the ensuing offspring became the Nephilim of myth and legend. The reality of who these ancient giants were, where they came from, and what ultimately happened to them is preserved in many world mythologies. For this reason, mythology can offer clues to a forgotten chapter in human history. As theologian Francis A. Schaeffer points out:

> More and more we are finding that mythology in general, though greatly contorted, very often has some historic base. And the

interesting thing is that one myth which occurs over and over again in many parts of the world is that somewhere a long time ago supernatural beings had sexual intercourse with natural women and produced a special breed of people. (Thomas 1986, 107)

THE ANUNNAKI AND NEPHILIM SAGA

Here we look to the Babylonian creation story, the *Enûma Eliš,* for greater insight into these matters. According to late author and independent researcher Zecharia Sitchin, the world was once ruled by a race of giants known in the *Enûma Eliš* as the Anunnaki. These beings were not earthborn creatures, but rather were extraterrestrial beings who came to Earth to mine for gold and "other precious raw minerals." In ancient Sumern the name means, literally, "Those Who from Heaven to Earth Came."

Ancient alien theorists see ancient Sumer as the greatest source of evidence of extraterrestrial intervention in the evolution of the human species and its civilization.* In 2010, the phenomenal History channel launched a brand new series, *Ancient Aliens,* that examines evidence of alien contact in the remote human past. It proposes that extraterrestrials visited a backward humanity, barely out of the Stone Age, and imbued it with knowledge of civilization. They impregnated our infant race with technologies and cultural constructs now considered to be foundational to our ancient civilizations, including: megalithic architecture (or what David Hatcher Childress calls "Atlantean construction"); advanced science and medicine; organized religious cults and methods of spiritual healing; and even modes of aerial transportation and weapons of warfare—hundreds of millennia ahead of our own time.

---

*While proponents of the race of giants hypothesis regard the Sumern culture as one of the earliest recorded civilizations, it is not necessarily considered to be extraterrestrial in origin (although it is assumed that it was preceded by a number of very advanced but lesser-known cultures stretching back into humankind's remote past).

The reign of the Anunnaki marks the beginning of the historic period in the legacy of the ancient giants. The Hebrew rendering of the name Anunnaki is Anakim, meaning "giants," a name that befits their gigantic stature as well as their technological sophistication. Anakim is another name for the Hebrew Nephilim. "The Nephilim were upon the Earth in those days before the Deluge and thereafter too, when the sons of the Elohim cohabitated with the daughters of the Adam and they bore children unto them" (Sitchin, 152).

THE BOOK OF ENOCH AND
THE BOOK OF GIANTS

The story of the Flood in the Bible gives us an inkling of what life here on Earth may have been like before the global deluge. The Book of Genesis gives us only brief glimpses of that alternative world history, and contrasts drastically with the nonbiblical, evolutionary view of history now maintained as the established paradigm. The *nonevolutionary* world history is explored further and in much greater detail in the apocryphal works known as the Book of Enoch and the Book of Giants, two books only recently rediscovered that were not officially canonized as part of the Bible.

The Book of Enoch was discovered by Scottish adventurer James Bruce in the eighteenth century when, during an expedition to Africa, he came across a number of mysterious scrolls. Ethiopian priests explained they were sacred biblical texts not included in the Hebrew or Christian Bibles. Tantalized by such a possibility, Bruce made efforts to acquire copies and took them back to London to be examined and translated. These Ethiopian documents did not become widely known, however, until German orientalist and Protestant theologian August Dillmann translated the Book of Enoch into German (Däniken 2009).

The Book of Enoch is one of the best sources among the ancient pseudepigrapha texts for accounts of giants, even though it has not been placed within the official canon of either the early Hebrew Bible or the Greek Septuagint, which is the basis of our modern Christian Old Testament.

The Book of Giants is actually a portion of the Book of Enoch that was unknown until the mid-twentieth century, when excavations at the Qumran caves on the Dead Sea counted them among the Dead Sea Scrolls. This rich treasure trove consists of dozens of scrolls and hundreds of fragments. With the aid of the Manichaean religion, the Book of Giants spread throughout the Old World. Versions were translated into Syriac, Greek, Persian, Sogdian, Uighur, and Arabic. Each version took on a life of its own, however, given that every translation incorporated the various regional myths and legends of its host population (Childress 2010). They help provide context for Old Testament writings and the relatively new religion of Christianity—including the enigmatic "fallen angels" or *Nephilim,* also sometimes called the Watchers—giving further insight into the world as it was before the Flood.

The Book of Giants describes the antediluvian world as follows: "[These fallen angels] knew the secrets of [all things]. [At this time] sin was great on the earth. The wicked angels killed many people and begot giants [with mortal women]."

Biblical scholar John Williams Rogerson writes: "[According to] Genesis 6: 1–6, there the 'children of God' have intercourse with women, producing a race of *Nephilim,* 'mighty men that were old, men of renown'" (Davies and Rogerson, 204).

Further passages from The Book of Enoch describe the so-called Watchers: "Enoch 6–11 describes how these heavenly beings (all named) teach the women about spells, root cutting and plants, astrology, weapons of war, and cosmetics. The women give birth to giants, who turn to cannibalism and blood-drinking. The Earth cries out for help, and God orders the execution of the giants, the binding of the Watchers beneath the hill until the Day of Judgment, and thereafter in a fiery chasm" ("Christian Mythology" 2013). Such images as giants, blood drinking, astrology, spells, and root cutting have been far more influenced by pagan and Greek sources than by anything Hebrew. But nonetheless, the Book of Enoch fills in the tremendous gaps in biblical history that we have, unfortunately, inherited from Genesis.

These passages are echoed in the remaining portions of the book. Likewise, in Enoch 7:3–6, the daughters of men "became pregnant, and they bore great giants, whose height was three thousand ells [a Germanic form of measurement approximating the length of one man's arm] who summoned all the acquisitions of men. And when men could no longer sustain them, the giants turned against them and devoured mankind. And they began to sin against birds, and beasts, and reptiles, and fish, and to devour one another's flesh, and drink their blood. Then the earth laid accusation against the lawless ones." According to Enoch at least, it was this course of events that precipitated the Great Flood.

Given all of this, the key question becomes: Who then is Enoch? What relevance does he have to the existence of giants in the Old Testament? Enoch was the son of Jared, the seventh of the antediluvian rulers and one of the ten patriarchs of the pre-Flood Earth. Enoch is described in Jewish legend as "king over all men." In Genesis 5:21–24 Enoch is described only briefly then disappears from the canonized biblical record: "(21) When Enoch had lived 65 years, he became the father of Methuselah, (22) Enoch walked with God 300 years and had other sons and daughters. (23) Altogether, Enoch lived 365 years. (24) Enoch walked with God; then he was no more, because God took him away" (Däniken 2009).

Enoch is also known by different names by many different cultures: Saurid, Hermes, and Idris, among them. He, more than any individual, is responsible for the genesis of human culture and civilization. Some scholars, such as Taqi al-Din Ahmad ibn Ali ibn Abd al-Qadir ibn Muhammad al-Maqrizi in his work *Khitat,* even cite him as the builder of the Great Pyramid (Däniken 2009).

NOAH: HUMAN OR GIANT?

The figure of the biblical Noah is also a tantalizing and puzzling one. In the *Journal of Biblical Literature,* religious scholar John C. Reeves writes: "One relatively unexplored motif that can be observed in certain strands of early Jewish interpretation of the figure of Noah as 'Flood-hero' revolves around the question of his true lineage and identity" (1993, 110). Reeves asks, was Noah fully human, the legitimate seed of Lamech? Or was he in reality born of a bastard race of giants spawned through the miscegenation of the fallen Watchers and mortal women who terrorized and defiled the Earth from the epoch of Jared to the onset of the Great Flood? Though never directly addressed in the Hebrew Bible, it is clear in some extrabiblical sources the latter was most likely the case: that the Flood-hero Noah was, in all probability, a giant.

This fascinating motif is first introduced in the *Genesis Apocryphon,* one of the Dead Sea Scrolls, wherein Lamech is confronted by the suspicion that his newborn boy Noah is not legitimately his son. He suspects that Noah, rather than being a pure human, is in fact the byproduct of a union between his wife, Batenosh, and one of the angelic Watchers: "Then I considered whether the pregnancy was due to the Watchers and Holy Ones . . . and I grew perturbed about this child. Then I, Lamech, became afraid and went to Batenosh [my wife . . . saying,] Everything will you truthfully tell me . . . you will tell me without lies . . . you will speak truthfully to me and not with lies" (1QapGen 2:1–7).

Batenosh then reassures Lamech that Noah is indeed pure of blood: "I swear to you by the Great Holy One, by the Ruler [of Heaven] that this seed is yours, that this pregnancy is from you, that from you is the planting of [this] fruit . . . [and that it is] not from any alien, or from any of the Watchers, or from any heavenly being . . . I tell you this truthfully" (1QapGen 2:14–18).

Lamech, however, doubts Batenosh's truthfulness. He is therefore compelled to seek counsel from his grandfather Enoch "to learn from him the truth of the whole matter" (Reeves 1993; 1QapGen 2:22).

Lamech consults with his grandfather, who then speaks to his son, Methuselah (Lamech's father), as we read in 1 Enoch 106:18 and 107:2: "And now make known to your son Lamech that the one who has been born is truly his son. And call his name Noah. . . . And now, my son go make known to your son Lamech that this child who has been born is truly his son, and (this) is no lie" (Reeves 1993).

Why then did Lamech suspect that something was wrong? This was due to the child's strange and supernatural appearance when he was born. His body was "white like snow and red like the flower of a rose, and the hair of his head (was) white like wool . . . and his eyes (were) beautiful, and when he opened his eyes, he made the whole house bright like the sun so that the whole house was exceptionally bright." This seems almost extraterrestrial.

It also said upon his entrance into the world, the newborn spoke. Lamech was afraid of the infant and ran to his father, Methuselah, saying, "I have begotten a strange son; he is not like a man, but is like the children of the angels of heaven, of a different type, and not like us" (Reeves 1993). While some attribute his unique countenance to being marked as an agent of God, others, Reeves included, suggest another angle entirely. There is in fact strong evidence to support the conclusion that Noah was a "giant."

In a third text, from the so-called *Pseudo-Eupolemus* we read:

Eupolemus in his work *On the Jews* says that those who were rescued from the Flood first founded the Assyrian city of Babylon. They were giants (and) built the recorded Tower. When it collapsed due to the action of God, the giants dispersed over the whole earth. In some anonymous writings we discover that Abraham traced his lineage to the giants. When these (giants) were living in Babylonia, they were slain by God on account of their impiety. One of them, Belos, escaped death (and) settled in Babylon, and after building a tower lived in it. It was called Belos after its builder Belos.

Given that Abraham was descended from Noah, it is here we see the clear affirmation that Belos was another name for Noah, and that this person was indeed a giant. His postdiluvian descendants settled in Babylon and were responsible for the building of the Tower of Babel. They were then dispersed across the face of the planet after the Lord confounded their language.

Why then was it so important for the *Genesis Apocryphon* and the Book of Enoch to prove his *human* lineage? Simply because there had already been a tradition of Belos, or Noah, being a giant that had gone back thousands of years (the *Pseudo-Eupolemus*), and it was important to establish the new biblical tradition of Noah being simply a human agent of God, and in that, to silence the critics and ultimately terminate any further speculation regarding the matter as to whether or not Noah was of the race of giants. With this accomplished, any knowledge of the actual truth was effectively killed (Reeves 1993; Chouinard 2011).

Throughout this chapter we have sought to provide some sense of what the Earth and its inhabitants may have been like in the ages before the Great Flood. That we have been only partially successful may be due to the fact that the fascinating records of this time contain accounts of strange creatures difficult for the modern mind to fully imagine. One thing is clear, however: The frequency of similar accounts of beings enormous in size might suggest that we should be more apt to accept their common consensus as common truth: giants, whether they were the Nephilim or other races of gigantic beings, did, at one point in the early development of humans, inhabit the Earth. Given this, we can only speculate what wondrous discoveries await us with regard to unearthing and further understanding the fantastic phenomenon of giants through time.

Next we will be taking on a very intriguing aspect of our general discussion: the evidence for giants in the ancient culture of Atlantis and how they may have had a hand in its demise.

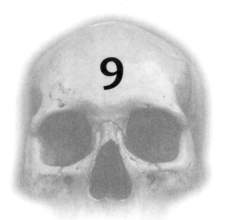

THE GREAT FLOOD
AND THE DESTRUCTION
OF THE GIANTS

THE FLOOD AND FLOOD LEGENDS

As Graham Hancock promptly notes at the beginning of his epic work *Underworld: The Mysterious Origins of Civilization,* millions of square kilometers of "useful human habitat" equivalent to all of China and Europe combined were "swallowed up by rising sea-levels at the end of the Ice Age" (2002, 24). Proof for this reality, Hancock insists, is all around us.

Descriptions of a cataclysmic worldwide flood, Hancock demonstrates, are present in nearly every culture on Earth. This tradition is seen in the Sanskrit writings of India, in the pre-Columbian Americas, and even in the works of the ancient Greeks. It is also prevalent in both Sumern and Babylonian written records, and among the prehistoric ancestors of the Celtic and Germanic tribes including the ancient Britons. We find flood myths among the Polynesian and Micronesian islanders, the Arabs, the Hebrews, and throughout China and Southeast Asia. Even in remote mountainous regions and scorching desert landscapes, far from the presence of any substantial body of water, flood myths persist. They speak of a major catastrophe that killed almost everyone alive on the planet at that time. No one, according to the records, but a select few escaped the onslaught of the torrent (Hancock 2002).

In this chapter we will look at these flood myths more closely and see what they can tell us about how giants might have been part and parcel of this ancient landscape.

A BIBLICAL ACCOUNT OF THE FLOOD

Graham Hancock remarks that in 1923 the noted anthropologist Sir James Frazer presented a commentary regarding the ever-present flood myths. Frazer was the author of the seminal work *The Golden Bough,* a collection of observations regarding folk practices and beliefs worldwide. Regarding prehistoric flood myths he said the following:

> Legends of a great flood in which almost all men perished are widely diffused over the world. . . . Stories of such tremendous cataclysms are almost certainly fabulous; [but] it is possible and indeed probable that under a mythical husk many of them hide a kernel of truth; that is they may contain reminiscences of inundations which really overtook particular districts, but which in passing through the medium of popular tradition have been magnified into worldwide catastrophes. (Hancock 2002)

Whether the biblical account of the Flood is merely a reminiscence of a local inundation or reflects a worldwide catastrophe, it is notable to us for other reasons, particularly concerning the issue of giants. Let's look at one biblical reference in particular to ascertain what may be a kernel of truth in it regarding our conviction that giants once peopled the Earth. This involves Noah's attempt to warn those around him of the coming catastrophe. They respond by saying "However great this deluge, we are so tall that it cannot reach our necks" (Joseph 2002, 119). This reference seems to echo the fact that they were indeed giants.

Author Frank Joseph goes on to identify more concisely the events preceding the Great Flood by noting that they appear to have been both seismic and celestial: "Earth shook, her foundations trembled, the sun darkened, lightning flashed, thunder pealed, a deafening voice the like of which was never heard before rolled across mountain and plain" (Joseph 2002, 119). Massive earthquakes followed by a dust-veil event and celestial explosions caused unprecedented chaos—death, destruction, floods, and conflagrations—in every corner of the globe. Joseph suggests that these effects are explained when God "opened Heaven's sluices by the removal of two Pleiades; thus allowing the Upper and Lower Water—the male and female elements of Tehom, which He had separated in the days of Creation—to re-unite and destroy the world in a cosmic embrace" (Joseph 2002, 119).

Joseph points out that in this passage "it is apparent that although the Heavenly Father punished mankind chiefly through the agency of water, He also 'rained fire on the evil-doers.'" Joseph continues:

Many existing and pre-existing cultures such as the Hebrews of the Middle East and the Aztecs of Mexico associate the Pleiades constellation with rain and floods. This connection goes back hundreds of thousands of years to the dimmest chapter of human antiquity. The planet Earth is pummeled by two massive meteors drawn from the Pleiades as instigated by the will of Yahweh.

Later in the Old Testament the full onslaught of this catastrophe is ultimately revealed. In Psalm 18:7–16, the effects of a massive cosmic collision and ensuing flood are described: Then the Earth did shake and quiver. The fountains of the mountains shook and spilled over because He was angry. His wrath steamed in billows of black smoke, and His face all fire, from which coals fell. He bent the very heavens in coming down, while he soared upon the very wings of the wind. He covered Himself in a dark cloud. Out of the blackness of this cloak rained hailstones, flaming coals. The Lord bellowed thunderously high in the heavens. Then channels of the deep waters were seen and the foundations of the Earth lay bare. Yet, he rescued me out of the great waters. (Joseph 2002, 120)

DEUCALION'S FLOOD

Another account of great significance in our quest to understand the history and mythology of ancient giants is the classical myth of Deucalion's flood, which describes a catastrophic worldwide extinction. In this myth, as with Plato's account of Atlantis, the flood was accompanied by violent storms, earthquakes, and avalanches. The watery abyss covered the entire Earth, with only the highest peaks protruding through the thrashing waters as islands in a newly cleansed and rejuvenated world.

In the classic account, Earth's life-forms passed through several ages. While Zeus is credited for at least one of the deluges, some versions indicate that at least five floods swept the Earth in the history of humanity. Each flood happened in a separate age. This idea supports the idea of the cyclical birth, death, and rebirth of civilizations. It might also help explain the conflicting evidence with regard to dating the Great Flood.

The Greek myth of Deucalion is different in some ways from the biblical account of the Flood, in which a breeding pair of every species created by God is stored in the Ark. According to the Bible, God instructed Noah to do this so that the animals, along with Noah's family, could survive the torrent and then repopulate the globe when the waters subsided. In the myth, all life is exterminated by the flood but for two survivors: the Titan giants Deucalion and Pyrrha. They took refuge in an ark (as with the biblical counterpart), which ran aground on a high mountain. After the waters receded they looked about in amazement. The planet was a barren, desolate, mud-covered world, a sight that modern readers could compare to the surface of the planet Mars. It was utterly devoid of living things.

The giants were instructed by the goddess Themis how to repopulate the Earth. "Throw the bones of your mother behind you" was her cryptic commandment. Deucalion and Pyrrha, being earthborn giants, concluded that the "bones of your mother" must be the rocks and boulders of Mother Earth that littered the ground. Deucalion picked up large boulders with his massive hands and tossed them over his shoulders. Before his very eyes, he saw the rocks turn to bone and the mud to flesh. Thus, one by one, new life evolved. Some of these creatures resembled older forms, while others were unique to the newly dawned epoch.

THE SUMERN FLOOD MYTH

In the Sumern flood myth, the gods decided to destroy the human race. The Priest-King Ziusudra was forewarned of the coming disaster by the god Enlil, and by his command, Ziusudra was to construct an immense ship, or ark, and assemble a male and female from each animal species and store them on the great craft.

This he did and soon there came a violent windstorm; the waters rushed forth and submerged the world beneath the tempestuous seas. The downpour continued unabated for seven days and nights. Finally, Ziusudra opened a window in the ark. The light from the blazing sun touched his face with warmth and comfort. He fell down on his knees, and prayed to the sun god Utu. He eventually landed on a now sunken landmass in the Persian Gulf. At this moment, he offered blood sacrifices to Anu and Enlil in the form of a sheep and an ox. Ziusudra was granted the gift of eternal life for his success in preserving the human race and the other creatures of the Earth, for returning life back to its usual order.

The similarity between this and a thousand other accounts, including the biblical story of Noah's Ark, are obvious, and notably redundant. It goes without saying that either there is a single original source from which all these myths derive or there is something much more profound at work here, namely that various cultures experienced the same massive event, and they all wrote about it, giving us these similar accounts. Today we all share, through the collective unconscious, memories of this Great Flood—only by and large we have forgotten it.

Along these lines, author Graham Hancock and noted scholar Hertha von Dechend both have worked extensively on the phenomenon of racial memory and amnesia. What this author wishes to emphasize is that those suppressed or forgotten memories reflect a past that is vastly different from modern life as we know it to be. A key difference, of course, revolves around a single crucial issue: that of giants being an integral part of the ancient landscape.

THE BABYLONIAN FLOOD MYTH

The Babylonian flood myth is very similar to the Sumern, Assyrian, and Hebrew accounts, with a number of significant differences. First of all, the Babylonian version proposes an ongoing cycle of destruction and renewal divided into three separate phases. Every 1,200 years the gods became upset, not with people's evils, but rather with the problem of overpopulation. During the first of these destructive phases, a virulent plague infected and killed off the human race. In the second phase the human race perished from hunger and malnutrition. The third and last phase was marked by a great flood, or deluge, that submerged every speck of land and drowned the human race in a deep, watery grave.

However, this was not the end of humanity's tenure on this planet, for the god Enki told Atrahasis to build a massive ship, or ark, so that he could escape together with his family and a collection of cattle, wild animals, and birds. Soon the sky turned black and the storm god Adad ravaged the land. After the deluge, Atrahasis prayed to the gods and offered up blood sacrifices in their honor. A covenant was made between the gods and humans, and infertility and stillborn births were introduced to humanity to ward off repeated periods of overpopulation. This is an interesting twist to the usual story, which always blames the gods' actions on humanity's wickedness, a position that would no doubt sit well among the mythologies and beliefs of our own modern age.

ASSYRIAN FLOOD MYTHS

In Assyrian tradition, we see more variations on the original Sumern and Babylonian themes, including the need to depopulate an overpopulated world. The god Enlil became aware of this overpopulation and harnessed the support of the other gods, and together they decided to send a flood to destroy humankind. Utnapishtim, the Assyrian Noah, had a dream in which the god Ea forewarned him of the coming deluge.

PHAETON AND THE GREAT FLOOD

In Greek mythology, the Great Flood is linked to Phaeton, the illegitimate son of Helio, the god who drove the blazing sun atop a chariot across the heavens. Phaeton demanded the opportunity to command the chariot himself, only to falter and lose control of the mighty horses, plummeting to Earth with disastrous consequences. As they hurtled perilously down to the planet, they burned forests into deserts and set vast prehistoric metropolises such as Atlantis on fire. Only Gaia, the Mother Earth goddess, elicited relief with her prayers for salvation. This came in the form of Zeus to the rescue. He hurled one of his mighty thunderbolts at Phaeton, thereby turning his chariot into flames. At this point, the chariot broke into pieces and bombarded the Earth with fireballs, where they crashed into the oceans, causing them to rise and flood the land in what was almost a total worldwide flood.

Not only is there evidence for this in some surviving monuments and in the rich diversity of cultural and mythological stories worldwide, there are strange, anomalous structures and sunken ruins in the oceans of the world that date back to a time when mainstream scientists claim cities did not exist.

OTHER FLOOD MYTHS

The Aztecs and Mayas believed that the world has gone through many cycles, or eras, which the Aztecs called "Suns." According to their culture, this pattern will continue onward, with each cycle ending with invasions of fire and water. In the Sanskrit writings of India, a successive number of creations are identified, after which everything in existence is destroyed by the converging waters; in the aftermath, these waters form a new ocean in which the next major creation will take place (Mahabharata 3.188.80, 3.189.42).

The cyclical periods of creation and destruction are part of a larger spiritual phenomena known as the Hindu yuga cycles, the current one being the Kali Yuga, which in contrast to the previous incarnations, is one of iniquity and chaos. Atlantologist Kenneth Caroli tells us that, with regard to the Mahabharata and the Hindu yuga cycles:

Interpreting the Hindu Yugas can be exceedingly difficult when trying to link each cyclical epoch to a western chronology. The dates for the rise and fall of Atlantis, for example, and the related deluge, are strictly conjectural but Blavatsky's Theosophists set it against the Davpara Yuga, the Bronze Age that preceded the current Kali Yuga. While traditionalist Hindus began Kali Yuga in 3102 BCE it was also the death of Krishna that genealogies put at ca. 1900–1400

BCE. Other interpretations have placed it as late as 700 BCE. Of course it remains an open question whether Atlantis is to be found in Hindu lore at all despite fervent attempts by Atlantists since the 19th century to find it there. Phonetic similarities between *Atlantis* and *Atala* may be more due to the relationship of Vedic and Greek languages. Incidently there was a Greek empire in nearby Bactria [mainly Afghanistan and some of Pakistan] in the 4th–2nd centuries BCE. Plato's writings might well have circulated there as well. The common link to Atlantis must be the Parthians and later Sassanids. The neo-Platonists fled to the Sassanid empire when Justinian shut down the Academy in 529 CE. (Caroli 2011)

In addition to the yuga cycles of India, many myths from cultures all around the world speak of massive floods that destroyed a lost civilization.

Some of the most well-known flood myths to Westerners are the biblical and Qur'anic flood myths involving Noah's Ark, the Greek Deucalion flood myth, and the *Epic of Gilgamesh,* a Mesopotamian poem dating to the eighteenth century BCE. In each myth there are always a select few who survive the torrent to rebuild civilization and repopulate the Earth. In most mythical stories, a great flood is sent by the gods, often as an act of divine retribution for various sins committed by human society, such as when Zeus became angered at the ancient Greeks for their insufferable acts of cannibalism and human sacrifice. In most cases such deluges are merely preludes to a mass extinction or end of the world. There are many other lesser-known examples.

In a more obscure flood myth, the god Faro of the Bambara people of Mali holds back the deluge that will someday come crashing forth to drown the present world in preparation for the new world that is about to rise. Knowledge of the coming catastrophe has been issued so that people may prepare by arming themselves with objects capable of imbuing them with eternal salvation.

Iranian texts speak of the coming snows and floods that will cover the Earth at the final moments of the cosmic millennium. In response to this terrible future, Yima comes forth, gathers the best races of humanity, and descends inside the Earth to await the millennial destruction. He then surfaces from his underground sanctuary and repopulates the world (Vendidad 2, 22–41).

There is no question that mythology plays a major role in the quest for humanity's ancient mysteries. But is this mythology supported by tangible evidence? Indeed, archaeology has provided a wealth of evidence that shows that our history goes back hundreds of thousands of years—a time frame mainstream science doesn't even acknowledge. Archaeology also provides clues to more recent origins. From the Mediterranean to the southern coast of Japan, archaeologists and independent researchers are finding cities that have been submerged for thousands of years, since the last ice age. Also, newer discoveries place some of the earlier submerged settlements at 8000–5000 BP.

The sunken cities and submerged ruins of the world provide an excellent opportunity to view human history from an entirely new perspective, and ultimately shed light on some of the imaginative flood myths and legends that have become such a vital part of our culture. More important, by coming to understand these various myths that exist the world over, it becomes possible to see what role the giants of old may have played in the drama depicting this most ancient of cataclysms.

The Great Flood was a catastrophic event in the distant past. We will now look at another one: the mystery of Atlantis and its destruction.

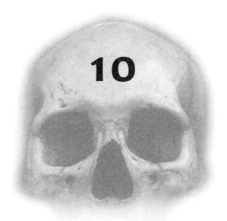

GIANTS OF ATLANTIS

The Greek Tradition

Now in this island of Atlantis there was a great and wonderful empire which had rule over the whole island and several others, and over parts of the continent and, furthermore, the men of Atlantis had subjected the parts of Libya within the columns of Heracles as far as Egypt, and of Europe as far as Tyrrhenia. This vast power, gathered into one, endeavored to subdue at a blow our country and yours and the whole of the region within the straits, and then, Solon, your country shone forth, in the excellence of her virtue and strength, among all mankind.

PLATO, *TIMAEUS*

I would have you call to mind the strength of the ancient giants, that undertook to lay the mountain Pelion on the top of Ossa, and set among those the shady Olympus.

FRANÇOIS RABELAIS, *WORKS, BOOK IV* [1548], CH.38

Author and explorer David Hatcher Childress correctly observed that more books have been written about Atlantis than any other subject (*Ancient Aliens* 2011). The mystery of Atlantis has become the embodiment of humankind's search for the unusual and unexplained. Whether you are a skeptic or a true believer, this theme resonates with a larger audience today than ever before. It seems to strike some primal chord deep within our psyche. *We know that we came from somewhere else.* Even if the mystery of Atlantis is never fully solved, 2,500 years of speculation and theory have provided a rich mythological backdrop for future discoveries.

The popularity of Atlantis is largely due to the writings of the Greek philosopher Plato. In two of his famous dialogues, the *Timaeus* and the *Critias,* he describes its culture and geography, its military exploits, and its relations with foreign powers. Finally, he concludes his account with the destruction of Atlantis in 9600 BCE.

In 600 BCE, Plato's ancestor, the Athenian statesman Solon, visited the city of Sais in Egypt and met with the Egyptian priesthood. There he learned of a unique connection between their two countries, even rumors that Egypt originally seeded Greek civilization. In the *Timaeus,* we read: "This city [Sais] was founded by a goddess whose name was 'Neith' in Egyptian (according to the people there) 'Athena' in Greek" (Jowett and Harward 1952, 443). According to Plato's account, Solon then began to recount his knowledge of ancient history. He discussed "Phoroneus—the first human being" and told the priests "the story of how Deucalion and Pyrrha survived the flood."

Solon went on to recount important Greek events and dates of the past. One of the priests was quick to interrupt him, saying: "Ah, Solon, Solon you Greeks are forever children. You don't even know your own history" (Jowett and Harward 1952, 447). Solon was told that there were past ages of such wonder that he could scarcely imagine them.

Solon then accepted their invitation to see the ancient records, which, they claimed, would tell him the secrets of a lost civilization, more ancient and mighty than the great Corinthian city-state Helike or powerful Troy combined. They brought Solon to a nearby temple and showed him ancient hieroglyphs inscribed on a stone column.

One priest read the words while another translated into Greek. This sacred knowledge was then passed on to Solon's cousin Dropides. Later, Plato heard these stories from his great-grandfather Critias, who was a direct descendant of Dropides. Plato then copied them down as his great-grandfather told them. Plato's two dialogues, the *Timaeus* and the *Critias,* were based on that Egyptian story told to Solon.

The *Timaeus* presents a general description of Atlantis, outlines its rulers' plans to conquer the entire known world, and details how the Athenians thwarted this act of aggression. The defeat of Atlantis foreshadowed the disaster to come. Shortly after, the entire continent and all its inhabitants sank beneath the waves, never to return. The *Critias* provides a detailed account of Atlantean society and describes how Atlantis was founded. The dialogue further explains how Atlantis evolved into a near-perfect society, only to be eventually destroyed.

In the *Timaeus,* the priest offers this piece of history, thousands of years in the past:

> There was an island opposite the strait that you call the Pillars of Hercules, an island larger than Libya and Asia combined; from it travelers could in those days reach the other islands, and from them the whole opposite continent that surrounds what can truly be called the ocean. On this island of Atlantis has arisen a power-ful and remarkable dynasty of kings. . . . Their wealth was greater than that possessed by any previous dynasty of kings or likely to be accumulated by any that would follow, and both in the city and countryside they were provided with everything they could require. Because of the extent of their power they received many imports, but for most of their needs the island itself provided.
>
> It had mineral resources from which were mined both solid mate-

rials and metals, including one metal which survives today only in name, but was then mined in quantities in a number of localities in the island, orichalc, in those days the most valuable metal except gold. There was a plentiful supply of timber for structural purposes and every kind of animal domesticated and wild, among them numerous elephants. For there was plenty of grazing for this largest and most voracious of beasts, as well as for all creatures whose habitat is marsh, swamp and river, mountain or plain. Besides all this, the earth bore freely all of the aromatic substances it bears today. . . . There were cultivated crops. . . . There were the fruits of trees. . . . All these were produced by their sacred island, then still beneath the sun, in wonderful quality and profusion. (Hancock 1992, 320)

But this grandiose civilization was not to last forever. Its climactic end can be considered the most enduring legacy of this ancient account. It inspired generations of well-traveled explorers and armchair theorists to rediscover the lost city of Atlantis, at least in their own imaginations.

One such speculative theory about Atlantis was formulated by Giorgio A. Tsoukalos, Erich von Däniken's business partner and associate in the United States. He suggests a possible UFO connection to the Atlantis mystery. Tsoukalos believes that Atlantis was never a stationary landmass at all, but rather a massive UFO or floating city. Contrary to historic accounts, the legendary city was never destroyed; instead, it launched itself back into space in a burst of fire and smoke, generating massive oceanic turmoil in its wake. This corresponds directly to Plato's account. Tsoukalos supports this notion by citing ancient legends that talk about floating cities that descended from the heavens, appearing suddenly and without warning. Then, just as quickly as they arrived, the mysterious floating cities once more aimed for the stars, returning to the home of the gods (*Ancient Aliens* 2011).

TECHNOLOGY VERSUS MYTH

If the city of Atlantis truly launched itself into the heavens as Tsoukalos posits, then clearly ancient technology was far more advanced than mainstream thinking allows. Is it only now that our own scientific understanding has progressed that we can begin to unravel what truly happened in the past?

In *Technology of the Gods,* David Hatcher Childress writes:

> As our technology has gotten more advanced, we have become able to look into the future and into outer space with a view different from that of scientists and thinkers earlier in this century. Similarly, we are now able to look at the past with greater insight and technological know-how. Just as our minds have been able to imagine a future different from that which our grandfathers could envision, we are also able to see a past different from that of the scientists and experts of the turn of the century. (2000)

Our technology has certainly been a useful tool in deciphering mysteries of the past, but it is not the only conduit for speaking with the ancients. Mythology, in my estimation, is a far more powerful method. It is, of course, one that is psychologically—yes, even psychically—connected to a forgotten chapter in Earth's history. Every myth has within it certain properties that give us hints to a half-remembered past.

Let's now look again at one of the classical world's most enduring myths: that of the *Titanomachy,** the story of the epic battle fought over a ten-year period between the giant Titans and Olympians. In it we may mine clues to the mystery that was Atlantis.

---

*Also known as the Battle of the Titans, Battle of Gods, or The Titan War, the *Titanomachy* is a classical story of Greek mythology that recounts the mighty battles between the Titans and the Olympians, specifically the fight of Zeus and his siblings against their father, Kronos. Ultimately the Olympians won and Zeus lorded over the entire kingdom.

A WAR IN HEAVEN—THE TITANS
AND THE OLYMPIANS

According to the *Titanomachy*, in the beginning there was only Chaos, a great emptiness from which nothing could escape. Then from Chaos the first three immortal beings emerged: Gaea (Mother Earth); Tartarus, ruler of the Underworld; and Eros (Love) most noted for his divine beauty. Gaea then, without having intercourse, gave birth to another being, Uranus (Father Sky), who would become equal to her in importance, and surrounding her, created a home for the newly born race of immortal beings. During this initial phase in the evolution of the universe, Gaea also gave birth to Ourea (Mountains) and Pontus (Sea), both of whom would play a vital role in the emergence of human civilization.

Gaea then married Uranus and had three sets of children with him: the thirteen Titans. They were Helios, Oceanus, Coeus, Crius, Hyperion, Iapetos, Theia, Rhea, Themis, Mnemosyne, Phoebe, Tethys, and Kronos. Gaea and Uranus also created three Cyclopes: Brontes, Steropes, and Arges. Each Cyclopes was of course a giant and possessed but a single massive eye in the middle of its forehead. Like the Judaic Nephilim, they were excellent architects and craftsmen, and like the giants of Wagner's operas, they constructed the original home of the gods. The couple also sired three nonhumanoid giants named the *Hekatoncheires,* or hundred-armed giants: Kottos, Briareos, and Gyges. These awesome giants were fully equipped with fifty heads and fifty arms extending from each shoulder.

Uranus hated and reviled his offspring, and banished them to the dark reaches of the underworld. After Uranus thrust his children down to the underworld, they fell for nine days and nine nights. On the tenth day, they reached the twelfth level of Tartarus. Here the children would remain segregated from the world above, never to know the light of day or the warmth of the sun, in order that Uranus could reign for eternity.

This disturbed Uranus's wife, Gaea, and she persuaded her youngest son, Kronos, to ambush his father. Kronos did so, and wielding a sickle he severed his father's genitals and allowed fresh blood to trickle down to Gaea, who became impregnated with the crimson paste. She then gave birth to three further sets of children: the Erinyes, Giants, and Meliai. In the aftermath, Uranus's genitals were hurled into the sea, and the foam that was produced formed the goddess Aphrodite (Hard 2004).

As Robin Hard writes in *The Routledge Handbook of Greek Mythology*:

> The story of the mutilation of Uranus and his separation from Gaea has obvious cosmological implications; since the sky now rises high above the earth, it is suggested in the myths of many cultures that Earth and Sky, as the first couple or at least a primordial couple, must somehow have been drawn apart at a very early stage in the history of the world. This is often achieved in a gentler fashion than in the present story. In an ancient Egyptian myth, for instance, Shu, the personification of air, is said to have interposed himself between the earth-god Geb and the sky-goddess Nut to raise the latter's body high over that of her partner. Or in Maori myth, from far away in New Zealand, the union between the couple Ragni and Papa, the female Earth and male Sky, became the first source of life, but all that they brought forth remained imprisoned between them initially because they never relaxed from their embrace; so the first gods, who formed part of their offspring, consulted together and resolved that Tane, the god of forests and birds, should separate Rangi and Papa by using his body to hold them apart; and when he did so light appeared in the world for the first time. (2004)

The implication of Kronos's mutilation of Uranus is clear. He was vying for a position of power among the highest order of the divine hierarchy. With his father safely deposed he, Kronos, ascended to the throne of authority. By doing so, he effectively became the complete master of creation.

Soon Kronos and his sister Rhea were married. They had five children; however, Kronos was warned by a witch that he would be murdered by one of his children. To solve this problem he swallowed each baby when it was born. But being immortal, the children did not perish; they simply remained alive and grew to maturity in Kronos's stomach cavity. When the sixth child was born, Rhea hid the child away and fooled Kronos by wrapping a massive stone in a blanket and giving it to him. He immediately gulped it down.

Meanwhile, the sixth child, Zeus, had been hidden away in a cave on Crete and was being raised by the nymphs. However, he was also preparing for the day of his great return to reclaim his birthright, for the Titans' reign on Earth was nearing a final end. Zeus rescued his brothers and sisters, the Olympians, from Kronos's stomach by slashing open their father's belly and releasing them. And then, with their help, Zeus usurped the power of the Titans and established a new pantheon of gods. However, despite his wounds Kronos remained alive, so after the Fall of the Titans, Zeus had his father Kronos chained, gagged, and locked away deep within the Earth.

Ruling over all the Earth from Mount Olympus, Zeus and his fellow deities would now command the cosmos forever. One of the giants' strongholds was the volcanic island of Phlegra. Scholars have often seen its eventual destruction as a metaphor for the destruction of a lost civilization, which may have been populated by humans of enormous size and even supernatural abilities (Caroli 2011).

Was Phlegra the lost civilization of Atlantis? There are many contenders for this role, and in our ensuing discussion we will examine many of them. We will also discuss where the survivors of Atlantis may have ended up once their beloved culture fell beneath the waves of the sea.

CONTENDERS FOR ATLANTIS

In an earlier version of the *Titanomachy,* Hesiod described a massive eruption occurring during Kronos's conflict with the Olympians. This may have depicted the eruption of Thera, a volcanic island in the southern Aegean, near Greece. It exploded in 1500 BCE. This catastrophic incident is often linked to events described in the biblical Exodus. The explosion is also suggestive of Plato's Atlantis account, and some conservative archaeologists insist that Plato's Atlantis was nothing more than a reinterpretation of this ancient cataclysm.

Another island that may have been the ancient Atlantis was Scheria—later to be known as the lands of the Phaeacians, where Odysseus was thrown after his captivity at the hands of the nymph Calypso. The people of Scheria originally dwelled with the Cyclopes, but after being oppressed under their tyranny for centuries, they migrated to the uninhabited isle and established a superior civilization. This was accomplished under the leadership of their wise king Nausithous.

In the days of the Argonauts, Scheria became Phaeacia and was ruled by a race of giants. Some later scholars have directly linked this island to Plato's Atlantis myth, citing the rationale that, similar to the Atlantean tradition, the Phaeacians worshipped the mighty sea god Poseidon.

Another sunken civilization that deserves consideration as possibly being the mysterious Atlantis is the lost civilization of Helike, a Greek city-state founded during the Bronze Age. Positioned on the southwestern shore of the Gulf of Corinth, Helike was the principal member of a coalition of twelve Greek city-states known as the Achaean League. Helike was also highly expansionistic, establishing colonies in both Asia Minor and southern Italy. In 373 BCE a cataclysmic earthquake and tsunami nearly obliterated and then submerged this cultural and religious center.

Plato describes a Temple of Poseidon in Atlantis, considered to be the holiest of shrines, comparable only to the Temple of Solomon. Helike, likewise, hosted a sanctuary of the Helikonian Poseidon, which was famous throughout the classical world (Katsonopoulou 1999, 2002). The citizens of Helike and the Atlanteans shared this cultural tradition, which buttresses the argument that Helike may actually have been Atlantis.

Plato was approximately fifty-four years old when the tsunami engulfed Helike. Without question, he must have known about its great destruction and taken note of its key characteristics. The power wielded by Helike's ruler, the vast colonial ambitions, and the destruction by earthquake and flood make it a prime contender for Atlantis. Furthermore, the inhabitants of Helike had become morally bankrupt and defiled the Temple of Poseidon, which also links it to Atlantis (Katsonopoulou 1999, 2002). The city's destruction was thus associated with the wrath of the mighty sea god, who punished Helike for its misdeeds and sacrilege.

According to legend, Atlantis had many survivors who left their sinking homeland for places unknown. Where did they go? We will explore one theory in our next section below. It offers up a tantalizing idea as to where the root of all civilization may actually have originated.

DID THE FLEEING ATLANTEANS END UP IN SUMER?

The myth of Atlantis can be traced back to ancient Sumern culture. As Boston University geologist Dr. Robert M. Schoch notes in his book *Voyages of the Pyramid Builders,* the conventional view holds that civilization began in ancient Sumer around 3500 BCE—"our first taste of civilization," as Schoch calls it. He also mentions a Babylonian legend that says the Sumerns were not native to Mesopotamia, but rather arrived there from a distant, forgotten homeland after a long journey by sea across the Western Ocean (Atlantic Ocean).

If true, this shifts the emphasis away from Mesopotamia as the root of all civilizations. It suggests, rather, that Sumer got its culture from another source entirely. This means, in turn, that the entire human race possibly owes its culture to a far more ancient, and still unidentified, supercivilization.

Might this have been Atlantis?

SUNKEN CITIES IN THE MEDITERRANEAN

In his Lost Cities series, author David Childress links the flooding of the Mediterranean with the destruction of Atlantis. Although some of Childress's theories amount to nothing more than mere speculation, this one may not be so far off the mark.

According to Childress in his 1996 release, *Lost Cities of Atlantis, Ancient Europe and the Mediterranean*, twenty thousand years ago the Mediterranean was not a sea, but rather a fertile river valley. Centuries later, the valley was overcome by a great deluge, transforming it into a saltwater sea. According to Childress, hundreds of sunken cities remain undiscovered in the Mediterranean, their ruins resting on the bottom of the sea floor. A sudden change in Earth's oceans caused the deluge, he says, triggering a massive tsunami that drowned the continent of Atlantis in thousands of feet of water, and then flooded and obliterated Mediterranean cities and much of predynastic Egypt.

Archaeologists have recently discovered the ruins of Pavlopetri, a five-thousand-year-old town submerged off the southern Laconia coast of Greece. This may prove to be the inspiration for many of the pre-Platonic folk traditions describing a civilization that was submerged in prehistoric times. Discoveries at the underwater site include various buildings and temple structures, along with ceramics, dating habitation from the Final Neolithic period (mid–fourth millennium BCE) to the end of the Late Bronze Age (1100 BCE), a time frame that brackets the age of Atlantis, according to Atlantologist Ken Caroli (ScienceDaily 2009).

This town was part of the civilization that launched a thousand ships in the heroic literature of Homer's epics depicting the Trojan War and the return of Odysseus. It was also a major port at the time of Agamemnon, so its remains offer archaeologists deep insight into the overall workings of Mycenaean society, which dates to approximately 1600–1000 BCE (ScienceDaily 2009).

This unique maritime settlement was an operations hub for coordinated local and long-distance commerce. Dr. Jon Henderson told *ScienceDaily*: "This site is unique in that we have almost the complete town plan, the main streets and domestic buildings, courtyards, rock-cut tombs and what appear to be religious buildings, clearly visible on the seabed. Equally as a harbor settlement, the study of archaeological material we have recovered will be extremely important in terms of revealing how maritime trade was conducted and managed in the Bronze Age" (2009).

A *megaron*—a large rectangular hall—dating to the Early Bronze Age was discovered among the remains. Also included in the extensive ruins is what appears to be the first pillar crypt ever found. Two stone cist graves and a Middle Bronze Age pithos burial were also identified amid the crumbling edifices (ScienceDaily 2009).

Today, many question whether Atlantis ever existed or was merely a figment of Plato's imagination, for even in ancient times, many questioned the legitimacy of his claims. Even Aristotle doubted his teacher's account and wrote that he had never heard any mention of Atlantis prior to its appearance in Plato's dialogues. Aristotle's preeminence among ancient scholars makes him a valuable witness, for indeed, the Roman natural philosopher Pliny referred to Aristotle as "a man of supreme eminence in every branch of science" (King 2005, 108). He was highly regarded as an intellect of supreme quality and measure, perhaps rivaling Plato in this regard.

But regardless of whether Atlantis was real, its myth has come to embody the search for arcane knowledge about humanity's mysterious past. Other myths follow similar lines in our search for the truth. In addition, the same argument that is used to support the supposition that giants were real can be used with regard to Atlantis's veracity. These are the accounts that have come down to us, and when taken together, they form a consensus view, given the fact that they all share one common denominator: the giants who were part and parcel of our distant past.

To believe otherwise is to imply a colossal failure of our collective human imagination.

The Future Will Disclose the Truth about the Past

Without question we are experiencing a rebirth in the study of ancient giants. The presence of giants in human prehistory, and more important, their relationship to us, has become a hotly debated topic. New discoveries on a regular basis continue to prove that this is a story that is as vital to the study of human evolution as any of the prehistoric finds discovered throughout southern Africa. Included in the myths and folklore of indigenous cultures and in the hallowed scriptures of our modern-day churches, temples, and mosques, the archetype of the giant is inescapable.

One of the key arguments of this book is that our ancient ancestors possessed a higher order of civilization than our present global culture. Contrary to popular belief, our ancestors were not ignorant and simple-minded, but rather had very sophisticated and advanced technologies as well as a clear knowledge of astronomy, medicine, and engineering—among other disciplines. Our distant forebears were also excellent record keepers as well as credible witnesses to the unusual phenomena of what the modern mind would deem "the alternative history of early civilization." We have also seen, with the introduction of the cosmic ray theory discussed in chapter 2, how it is scientifically possible for radiation to cause mutations resulting in abnormally large beings.

However, as we know, we are immersed in a global conspiracy masterminded by the world's many national governments that suppresses many new discoveries that seek to confirm that we were, in actual fact, preceded by a race of giants. Because many of these anomalous discoveries have engendered controversy, they are often met with a "knowledge filter"—a self-limiting system that tends to dismiss new theories, not judging them on their merits, but instead rejecting them because they don't necessarily fit with what has become the standardized, codified knowledge base that establishment academics support (Gallegos 2009, 11). Given this, there is little chance of a truly original and paradigm-shattering idea ever gaining widespread acceptance within mainstream scientific circles. The guardians of the establishment simply don't want to risk their reputations and careers on a competing idea, even if that idea is the correct one. Rather than acting to support a genuine search for the truth, this filter relegates any and all ideas, evidence, or speculation not officially sanctioned by the academic hierarchy to the domain of "fringe science." This is a death sentence for any scientist attempting to gain broad acceptance for a new theory.

In contrast to current academic thought regarding the nature of human evolution, I believe in intelligent intervention, the idea that our evolution was accelerated five hundred thousand years ago by a targeted mutation of our genes by extraterrestrials. I also believe that giants represent the true earthborn race that evolved independently on this world, as a result of this mutation, over its four-billion-year history. This mutated culture is described in the Sanskrit writings of India; it possessed the Vimana spacecraft, and it was eventually either adopted by or passed on to the larger human population. All of this was to end during the great age of cataclysms, when Atlantis and the world trembled and then passed into oblivion.

My beliefs are contrary to those of most scientific elitists who support an absolutist interpretation of Darwin's theory and thus reject the concept of a targeted mutation and the ensuing development of a race of giants. Personally, however, I see no evidence that the race of giants hypothesis is incompatible with the theory of evolution as impacted by an alien intervention.

In the pages of this book I have attempted to present the argument for the race of giants theory and, in so doing, have provided ample evidence from the world over, whether that evidence is found in mythological accounts containing irrefutable references to giants or in findings unearthed in the archaeological record. There is no question in my mind that the findings from these excavations are genuine, as most if not all were unearthed within plain view of numerous, if not hundreds, of eyewitnesses. Many were widely documented at the time of their discovery.

The issue of prehistoric giants such as *Gigantopithecus* and *Meganthropus* is a closed case. Their existence is neither speculation nor some sort of hoax. There really were gigantic humanlike creatures living in the dense, tropical rain forests of Southeast Asia—as there probably are to this day! The established cry of lack of evidence might fit in well at academic-dominated universities or skeptical publications, but the plain truth of the matter is that evidence is robust and abundant, from documentary and historical data, to archaeological discoveries, to rich mythological traditions. We are approaching ever closer a real understanding of the remote human past and the mysterious creatures that shared this planet with us.

In this book, I the writer and you the reader have taken up an exploration of giants in the ancient world. I hope that what you have ingested here has opened your mind to the idea that giants were, in all probability, a seminal part of our remote past.

It is my belief that in the months and years ahead, more fossilized remains of giants will be unearthed throughout the world. As a result, the views of the mainstream establishment will be pushed to the tipping point, and it will be sheer folly to continue to refute what is the obvious truth: giants were a part of human evolution, and to them we owe an immeasurable debt in ways that may well prove too innumerable to ever fully calibrate.

Bibliography

Alexander, Robert E. 2005. "The Velikovsky Affair: Case History of Lac-
trogenic Behavior in Physical Science." *The Iatrogenic Handbook: A
Critical Look at Research and Practice in the Helping Professions.* Ed.
Robert F. Morgan. Fresno, Calif.: Morgan Foundation Publishers.

Allen, Joseph L., and Blake Joseph Allen. 2008. *Exploring the Lands of the
Book of Mormon.* Orem, Utah: Book of Mormon Tours and Research
Institute.

Andrews, Peter. 1974. *Christmas in Germany.* Chicago: World Book
Encyclopedia.

Authentic Artifact Collectors Association. www.theaaca.com/biocain4.htm
(accessed July 6, 2011).

Baumer, Christoph. 2000. *Southern Silk Road: In the Footsteps of Sir Aurel
Stein and Sven Hedin.* Bangkok: White Orchid Books.

Beckley, Timothy Green. 2009. *Giants in the Earth.* New Brunswick, N.J.:
Global Communications.

———. 2010. *The American Goliah—And Other Fantastic Reports of
Unknown Giants and Humongous Creatures.* New Brunswick, N.J.:
Global Communications.

Bellwood, Peter S. 1978. *The Polynesians: Prehistory of an Island People.*
London: Thames and Hudson.

Bulfinch, Thomas. 2004. *Bulfinch's Mythology: The Age of Fable or Stories of Gods and Heroes*. Sioux Falls, S.Dak.: NuVision Publications, LLC.

Callegari-Jacques, S. M., F. M. Salzano, J. Constans, et al. 1993. "Gm Haplotype Distribution in Amerindians: Relationship with Geography and Language." *Am J Phys Anthropol* 90, no. 4:427–44.

Caroli, Kenneth. 2011. Personal correspondence.

———. 2012. Personal correspondence.

Charles, R. H., and W. O. E. Oesterley. 1929. *The Book of Enoch*. London: Society for Promoting Christian Knowledge.

Chattaway, Peter T. "Giants in the Bible." http://peter.chattaway.com/articles/giants.htm (accessed May 1, 2013).

Childress, David Hatcher. 1988. *Lost Cities of Ancient Lemuria and the Pacific*. Stelle, Ill.: Adventures Unlimited Press.

———. 1991. *Lost Cities and Ancient Mysteries of the Southwest*. Kempton, Ill.: Adventures Unlimited Press.

———. 1996. *Lost Cities of Atlantis, Ancient Europe and the Mediterranean*. Stelle, Ill.: Adventures Unlimited Press.

———. 1998. *Lost Cities of China, Central Asia, and India*. 3rd ed. Kempton, Ill.: Adventures Unlimited Press.

———. 2000. *Technology of the Gods: The Incredible Sciences of the Ancients*. Kempton, Ill.: Adventures Unlimited Press

———. 2010. *Yetis, Sasquatch & Hairy Giants*. Kempton, Ill.: Adventures Unlimited Press.

Chouinard, Patrick C. 2008. *A Legacy of Gods and Empires: The Quest for Ancient Mysteries*. Clearwater, Fla.: Vanir House.

———. 2012. *Forgotten Worlds*. Rochester, Vt.: Bear & Company.

"Christian Mythology." 2013 http://en.wikiquote.org/wiki/Christian_mythology (accessed May 30, 2011).

Christmas, Jane. 2005. "Giant Ape Lived alongside Humans." *Daily News*, McMaster University, November 7. http://dailynews.mcmaster.ca/article/giant-ape-lived-alongside-humans/ (accessed May 1, 2013).

Däniken, Erich von. 1970. *Chariots of the Gods? Unsolved Mysteries of the Past*. New York: Putnam.

———. 2009. *History Is Wrong.* Franklin Lakes, N.J.: Career Press.

———. 2010. *Twilight of the Gods: The Mayan Calendar and the Return of the Extraterrestrials.* Pompton Plains, N.J.: New Page Books.

Davidson, Hilda Roderick Ellis. 1990. *Gods and Myths of Northern Europe.* Harmondsworth, U.K.: Penguin Books.

———. 1993. *The Lost Beliefs of Northern Europe.* London: Routledge.

Davies, Philip, and John Rogerson. 2006. *The Old Testament World.* Louisville, Ky.: Westminster John Knox Press.

de la Vega, Garcilaso. 1723. *Primera Parte de los Comentarios Reales.* Madrid, Spain: Nicolas Rodriguez Franco.

Diamond, Jared M. 1999. *Guns, Germs, and Steel: The Fates of Human Societies.* New York: W. W. Norton.

Dunbavin, Paul. 2003. *Atlantis of the West: The Case for Britain's Drowned Megalithic Civilization.* Rev. ed. New York: Carroll and Graf.

Fitzmyer, Joseph A. 1971. *The Genesis Apocryphon of Qumran Cave I.* Rome: Biblical Institute Press.

Flenley, John, and Paul G. Bahn. 2003. *The Enigmas of Easter Island: Island on the Edge.* Oxford: Oxford University Press.

Gallegos, F. 2009. "Beyond History: Alternative Historical Perspectives." Research Paper, San Jose State University.

gdub. 2012. "Evidence for Modern Humans in Americas 250,000 Years Ago!" Ancientstuff Forum, September 9. http://ancientstuff.maxforum.org/2012/09/09/evidence-for-modern-humans-in-americas-250000-year (accessed May 6, 2013).

Geoffrey of Monmouth, and Lewis G. M. Thorpe. 1966. *The History of the Kings of Britain.* Harmondsworth, U.K.: Penguin.

Gnostic Liberation Front. 2003. http://gnosticliberationfront.com/index.htm (accessed May 1, 2013).

Green, Matthew. 2005. "Red Headband of Comoros." Rich La Bonté, *eXoNews,* April 29. http://richlabonte.net/exonews/xtra/nonproliferation.htm (accessed May 1, 2013).

Grimm, Jacob. 1882. *Teutonic Mythology.* London: George Bell and Sons.

Guerber, H. A. 1895. *Myths of Northern Lands: Narrated with Special Reference to Literature and Art.* New York: American Book.

———. 1909. *Myths of the Norsemen: From the Eddas and Sagas.* London: George G. Harrap.

Gunther, John. 1955. *Inside Africa.* New York: Harper.

Hall, Mark A., and Loren Coleman. 2010. *True Giants: Is Gigantopithecus Still Alive?* San Antonio, Tex.: Anomalist Books.

Hancock, Graham. 1992. *The Sign and the Seal: The Quest for the Lost Ark of the Covenant.* New York: Crown.

———. 2002. *Underworld: The Mysterious Origins of Civilization.* New York: Crown.

Hard, Robin. 2004. *The Routledge Handbook of Greek Mythology.* London: Routledge.

Hendel, Ronald S. 1987. "When the Sons of God Cavorted with the Daughters of Men." *Bible Review* 3, no. 2.

———. 2009. "Giants at Jericho." *Biblical Archaeology Review* 35, no. 2 (March–April):20–21.

History. 2010. *Ancient Aliens: Season Two* (DVD). Narrated by Robert Clotworthy. New York: History.

———. 2011. *Ancient Aliens: Season Three* (DVD). Richard Monahan and Max Thompson, supervising producers. Narrated by Robert Clotworthy. New York: History.

History of Erie County, Pennsylvania. 1884. Vol. 1. Chicago: Warner, Beers and Co. http://theparanormalpastor.blogspot.com/2010/07/giant-indian-mound-builders-of-erie.html (accessed June 5, 2013).

Hitching, Francis. 1978. *Earth Magic.* New York: Pocket.

"Holocaust of Giants: The Great Smithsonian Cover-up." X-peditions Magazine.com. www.xpeditionsmagazine.com/magazine/articles/giants/holocaust.html (accessed May 1, 2013).

Huron Expositor Newspaper (Ontario, Canada). 1893. "Men of Great Stature Found at Two Large Burial Sites in Nebraska." October 13.

Joseph, Frank. 2002. *Lost Pyramids of Rock Lake: Wisconsin's Sunken Civilization.* Lakeville, Minn.: Galde Press, Inc.

———. 2005. *The Atlantis Encyclopedia.* Franklin Lakes, N.J.: New Page Books.

———. 2006. *The Lost Civilization of Lemuria: The Rise and Fall of the World's Oldest Culture.* Rochester, Vt.: Bear & Company.

———. 2010. *Advanced Civilizations of Prehistoric America: The Lost Kingdoms of the Adena, Hopewell, Mississippians, and Anasazi.* Rochester, Vt.: Bear & Company.

———. 2013. *Before Atlantis.* Rochester, Vt.: Bear & Company.

Jowett, Benjamin, and John Harward, trans. 1952. *The Dialogues of Plato.* Great Books of the Western World 7. Chicago: W. Benton.

Katsonopoulou, D. 1999. "Mycenaean Helike." *Meletemata: Studies in Aegean Archaeology Presented to M. Wiener as He Enters his 65th Year, Aegaeum* 20:409–13.

———. 2002. "Helike and Her Territory in the Light of New Discoveries." *Gli Achei e l'identita etnica degli Achei d'occidente.* Ed. E. Greco. *Tekmeria* 3:205–16.

King, David. 2005. *Finding Atlantis: A True Story of Genius, Madness and an Extraordinary Quest for a Lost World.* New York: Harmony Books.

Knight, Christopher, and Robert Lomas. 2001. *Uriel's Machine: Uncovering the Secrets of Stonehenge, Noah's Flood, and the Dawn of Civilization.* Gloucester, Mass.: Fair Winds Press.

Kolosimo, Peter. 1973. *Timeless Earth.* London: Garnstone Press.

Mackenzie, Donald A. 1912. *Teutonic Myth and Legend: An Introduction to the Eddas and Sagas, Beowulf, the Nibelungenlied, etc.* London: Gresham.

Maeir, A. M., S. J. Wimmer, A. Zukerman, and A. Demsky. 2008. "A Late Iron Age I/Early Iron Age II. An Old Canaanite Inscription from Tell es-Sâfi/Gath, Israel: Palaeography, Dating, and Historical-Cultural

Significance." Bulletin of the American Schools of Oriental Research 351:39–71.

Mayor, Adrienne. 2000. *The First Fossil Hunters: Paleontology in Greek and Roman Times*. Princeton, N.J.: Princeton University Press.

"Mysterious Giant Human Skeleton Discovered in Saudi Arabia." Friskodude. http://friskodude.blogspot.com/2004/06/mysterious-giant-human-ske_108818267252410645.html (accessed May 6, 2013).

Nettleton, Harvey. 1960. "History of Ashtabula County." *Geneva Times*. Nettleton's original account was written in 1844. http://solomonspalding.com/SRP/saga2/Ashtab1.htm#1844genev1 (accessed May 6, 2013).

Noorbergen, Rene. 1977. *Secrets of the Lost Races: New Discoveries of Advanced Technology in Ancient Civilizations*. Indianapolis: Bobbs-Merrill.

Norvill, Roy. 1979. *Giants: The Vanished Race of Mighty Men*. Wellingborough, U.K.: Aquarian Press.

Quayle, Stephen. 2002. *Giants: Master Builders of Prehistoric and Ancient Civilizations*. Genesis 6. Boseman, Mont.: End Time Thunder.

Reeves, John C. 1993. "Utnapishtim in the Book of Giants?" *Journal of Biblical Literature* 112, no. 1:110–15.

Rosenberg, Donna. 1994. *World Mythology: An Anthology of the Great Myths and Epics*. Lincolnwood, Ill.: NTC.

Routledge, Katherine. 2007. *The Mystery of Easter Island*. New York: Cosimo, Inc.

Sacks, David. 1995. *Encyclopedia of the Ancient Greek World*. New York: Facts on File.

Sagan, Carl. 1980. *Cosmos*. New York: Random House.

Schoch, Robert M. 2004. *Voyages of the Pyramid Builders*. New York: Jeremy P. Tarcher.

Schrag, Paul, and Xaviant Haze. 2011. *The Suppressed History of America: The Murder of Meriwether Lewis and the Mysterious Discoveries of the Lewis and Clark Expedition*. Rochester, Vt.: Bear & Company.

ScienceDaily. 2009. "World's Oldest Submerged Town Dates Back 5,000 Years." October 16, www.sciencedaily.com/releases/2009/10/091016101809.htm (accessed March 15, 2011).

Sitchin, Zecharia. 2010. *There Were Giants upon the Earth: Gods, Demigods, and Human Ancestry: The Evidence of Alien DNA.* Rochester, Vt.: Bear & Company.

St. John Daily News. 1878. "The Indian Chief Chickasawba: Skeletons Eight and Ten Feet in Height." September 13.

Steiger, Brad. 1978. *Worlds before Our Own.* New York: Berkley.

Stuckenbruck, Loren T., and Otto Betz. 1997. *The Book of Giants from Qumran.* Tübingen, Germany: Mohr Siebeck.

Thomas, I. D. E. 1986. *The Omega Conspiracy: Satan's Last Assault on God's Kingdom.* Oklahoma City: Hearthstone Publishing Limited.

Thompson, Lucy. 1991. *To the American Indian: Reminiscences of a Yurok Woman.* 1916. Reprint, Berkeley, Calif.: Heyday Books.

Time-Life. 1991. *Mysterious Lands and Peoples.* New York: Time-Life.

Troitsina, Margarita. 2011. "Cemetery of Giant Creatures Found in Central Africa." *Pravda,* June 24, http://english.pravda.ru/science/mysteries/24-06-2011/118302-giants_cemetery-0 (accessed May 6, 2013).

Vardanyan, Mihran. 2011. "Stars and Stones 2010: Oxford University Expedition to Qarahunge, Armenia." http://qarahunge.icosmos.co.uk (accessed May 6, 2013).

Way, Kenneth C. 2000. "Giants in the Land: A Textual and Semantic Study of Giants in the *Bible* and the Ancient Near East." Master's thesis, Trinity International University.

Weidenreich, Franz. 1946. *Apes, Giants, and Man.* Chicago: University of Chicago Press.

Wilkins, Harold T. 1947. *Mysteries of Ancient South America.* London: Rider.

———. 1952. *Secret Cities of Old South America.* Kempton, Ill.: Adventures Unlimited Press.

Williams, William W. 1878. *History of Ashtabula County, Ohio.* Philadelphia: Williams Brothers. See esp. chap. 6, "The Mound-Builders," by Stephen D. Peet. http://solomonspalding.com/SRP/saga2/1878Ast1.htm (accessed June 5, 2013).

Wright, G. Ernest. 1938. "Troglodytes and Giants in Palestine." *Journal of Biblical Literature* 57, no. 3:305–9.

INDEX